ACTIVITY

W9-BET-599

SIDE by SIDE

THIRD EDITION

BOOK 1

Steven J. Molinsky
Bill Bliss

with

Carolyn Graham • Peter S. Bliss

Contributing Authors

Dorothy Lynde • Elizabeth Handley

Illustrated by
Richard E. Hill

Longman

Side by Side, 3rd edition
Activity Workbook

Pearson Education, 10 Bank Street, White Plains, NY 10606

Vice president, director of publishing: *Allen Ascher*
Editorial manager: *Pam Fishman*
Vice president, director of design and production: *Rhea Banker*
Associate director of electronic production: *Aliza Greenblatt*
Production manager: *Ray Keating*
Director of manufacturing: *Patrice Fraccio*
Associate digital layout manager: *Paula D. Williams*
Interior design: *Wendy Wolf*
Cover design: *Elizabeth Carlson*

Illustrator: *Richard E. Hill*

The authors gratefully acknowledge the contribution
of Tina Carver in the development of the original
Side by Side program.

ISBN 0-13-026745-7

6 7 8 9 10 – CRK – 05 04 03

CONTENTS

A WHAT ARE THEY SAYING?

what's	is	my	from	name	phone number
where	are	your	I'm	address	

1. ___What's___ your name?

   My _____ is Janet Miller.

2. What's your _____?

   _____ address _____ 456 Main Street.

3. What's _____ phone number?

   My _____ _____ is 654-3960.

4. What's _____ name?

   My _____ is Ken Green.

5. _____ your address?

   My _____ is 15 Park Street.

6. What's your _____ number?

   _____ phone _____ is 379-1029.

7. _____ _____ you from?

   _____ _____ Detroit.

B NAME/ADDRESS/PHONE NUMBER

STUDENT IDENTIFICATION CARD

Name: <u>Maria</u>   <u>Gonzalez</u>
     First Name   Last Name

Address: <u>235 Main Street</u>

         <u>Bronx, New York</u>

Phone
Number: <u>741-8906</u>

*My name is Maria Gonzalez.
My address is 235 Main Street.
My phone number is 741-8906.*

How about you? What's YOUR name, address, and phone number?

STUDENT IDENTIFICATION CARD

Name: _____
     First Name   Last Name

Address: _____

_____

Phone
Number: _____

My name _____ ....

....

My _____ _____ ....

....

My _____ _____ _____

....

C LISTENING

Listen and circle the number you hear.

1. (5) / 9

2. 3 / 7

3. 1 / 2

4. 6 / 3

5. 4 / 1

6. 3 / 6

7. 5 / 4

8. 8 / 2

9. 10 / 0

10. 5 / 9

Activity Workbook   **3**

D NUMBERS

zero	0
one	1
two	2
three	3
four	4
five	5
six	6
seven	7
eight	8
nine	9
ten	10

Write the number.

four _____4_____

seven _____

one _____

eight _____

ten _____

two _____

nine _____

six _____

five _____

three _____

Write the word.

6 _____six_____

2 _____

7 _____

3 _____

1 _____

8 _____

10 _____

4 _____

9 _____

5 _____

E LISTENING

Listen and write the missing numbers.

1. What's your phone number?

My phone number is 389-793_2_ .

2. What's your telephone number?

My telephone number is 837-29___3.

3. What's your apartment number?

My apartment number is ___-B.

4. What's your address?

My address is ___ Main Street.

5. What's your fax number?

My fax number is 654-___ ___15.

6. What's your license number?

My license number is 26___3___9___ .

F LISTENING

Listen and write the missing letters.

1. C-A-_R_-T-___-R

2. J-O-___-N-___-O-___

3. ___-E-R-___-L-___

4. A-N-D-E-___-S-___-N

5. ___-H-I-L-___-I-P

6. ___-A-R-___-I-N-E-___

G WHAT ARE THEY SAYING?

name	meet	you	Hi	Nice

A. Hello. My ___name___ ¹ is Dan Harris.

B. _____ ². I'm Susan Wilson.

  Nice to _____ ³ you.

A. _____ ⁴ to meet _____ ⁵, too.

is	you	Hello	I'm	My	to

A. Hi. _____ ⁶ name _____ ⁷ Alice Lane.

B. _____ ⁸. _____ ⁹ Bob Chang.

A. Nice _____ ¹⁰ meet you.

B. Nice to meet _____ ¹¹, too.

H GRAMMARRAP: *Hi! Hello!*

Listen. Then clap and practice.

A. Hi. I'm Jack.

B. Hello. I'm Jill.

C. Hi. I'm Mary.

D. Hello. I'm Bill.

All. Nice to meet you.

  Nice to meet you, too.

A. Hi. I'm Bob.

B. Hello. I'm Tim.

C. Hi. I'm Susie.

D. Hello. I'm Jim.

All. Nice to meet you.

  Nice to meet you, too.

A PUZZLE

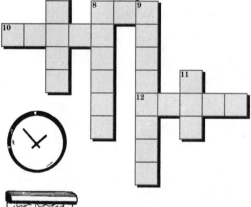

Across

1.

5.

6.

8.

10.

12.

Down

1.

2.

3.

4.

7.

8.

9.

11.

B LISTENING

Listen and put a check (✓) under the correct picture.

1. ✔ _____

2. _____ _____

3. _____ _____

4. _____ _____

5. _____ _____

6. _____ _____

C WHAT ARE THEY SAYING?

I'm	are	basement	attic	living room
we're	where	dining room	yard	bedroom
they're	you	kitchen	bathroom	

1. ___Where___ are you?

I'm in the _____.

2. Where _____ Susan and Joe?

_____ in the _____.

3. Where _____ you and Julie?

_____ in the _____.

4. _____ are you?

_____ in the _____.

5. _____ _____ Ben and Maria?

_____ in the _____.

6. Where _____ you and Betty?

_____ in the _____.

7. _____ _____ Pam and Peter?

_____ in the _____.

8. _____ _____ you?

_____ in the _____.

D WHAT ARE THEY SAYING?

where's	she's	classroom	garage	he's	living room	it's

1. _____Where's_____ David?

_He's_ in the _____.

2. _____ Millie?

_____ in the _____.

3. _____ the computer?

_____ in the _____.

E WHERE ARE THEY?

we	he	they
	she	
	it	

(Mr. and Mrs. Chen)   1. _____They_____ are in the kitchen.

(Ms. Carter)   2. _____ is in the dining room.

(Mr. Grant)   3. _____ is in the bathroom.

(Harry and Mary)   4. _____ are in the basement.

(Ellen and I)   5. _____ are in the attic.

(The bookshelf)   6. _____ is in the living room.

(Mr. White)   7. _____ is in the garage.

(Mrs. Miller)   8. _____ is in the classroom.

(The telephone book)   9. _____ is in the bedroom.

F WHERE ARE THEY?

I'm	we're	he's	where's
	you're	she's	
	they're	it's	

(He is)   1. _____He's_____ in the bedroom.

(They are)   2. _____ in the basement.

(We are)   3. _____ in the attic.

(I am)   4. _____ in the bathroom.

(It is)   5. _____ in the dining room.

(She is)   6. _____ in the living room.

(You are)   7. _____ in the garage.

(Where is)   8. _____ the cell phone?

G THE BAKER FAMILY

The Baker family is at home today. **(1)** Mrs. Baker is ___in___ ___the___ ___living___ ___room___ . **(2)** Mr. Baker is _____ _____ _____ . **(3)** Peggy and Jim are _____ _____ _____ . **(4)** Kevin is _____ _____ _____ . **(5)** Susie is _____ _____ _____ . **(6)** And the car is _____ _____ _____ .

H WHERE ARE THEY?

he's	they're
she's	
it's	

1. Where's Mrs. Baker?   <u>She's in the living room.</u>

2. Where's Mr. Baker?   _____

3. Where are Peggy and Jim?   _____

4. Where's Kevin?   _____

5. Where's Susie?   _____

6. Where's the car?   _____

1 WHAT'S THE SIGN?

Fill in the signs. Then complete the sentences.

1. Helen is _____in the park_____ .

2. Mr. and Mrs. Grant are _____
_____ .

3. Edward is _____ .

4. Maria is _____ .

5. Jim and Sarah are _____
_____ .

6. Billy is _____ .

7. The monkey is _____ .

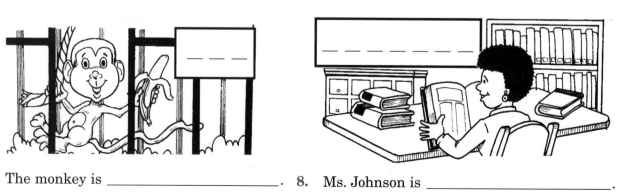

8. Ms. Johnson is _____ .

LISTENING

Listen and write the number under the correct picture.

SOCIAL SECURITY

_____

1

_____

_____

_____

_____

K **LISTENING**

Listen and circle the word you hear.

1.	zoo	(you)	3.	We're	They're	5.	Where	Where's	7. on in
2.	Ms.	Mr.	4.	Where	How	6.	She's	He's	8. Is It's

L **MATCHING**

Match the nationality and the city.

_c_ 1. We're Mexican. We're from _____.   a. Shanghai

____ 2. She's Greek. She's from _____.   b. San Juan

____ 3. He's Chinese. He's from _____.   c. Mexico City

____ 4. I'm Italian. I'm from_____.   d. Seoul

____ 5. They're Puerto Rican. They're from _____.   e. Athens

____ 6. We're Korean. We're from _____.   f. Tokyo

____ 7. She's Japanese. She's from _____.   g. Rome

M GRAMMARRAP: *Where's Jack?*

Listen. Then clap and practice.

A.	Where's	Jack?
B.	He's in the	kitchen.
A.	Where's	Jill?
B.	She's in the	dining room.
A.	Where's	Mom?
B.	She's in the	living room.
A.	Where's	Fred?
All.	Fred's in	bed.
	Fred's in	bed.
A.	Jack's in the	kitchen.
All.	Fred's in	bed.
A.	Jack's in the	kitchen.
B.	Jill's in the	dining room.
A.	Mom's in the	living room.
All.	Fred's in	bed.

Fred's in   bed.

N GRAMMARRAP: *Where Are Fred and Mary?*

Listen. Then clap and practice.

Where are   Fred and Mary

A.	Where's	Jack?	A.	Jack and	Jill.
B.	Where's	Jill?	B.	Betty and	Bill.
C.	Where are Fred and Mary?		C.	Bob and	Lou.
D.	Where's	Bill?	D.	Mary and	Sue.
A.	Where's	Ed?	A.	Jack and	Jill.
B.	Where's	Sue?	B.	Betty and	Bill.
C.	Where are Bob and	Betty?	C.	Bob and	Lou.
D.	Where are Tom and Lou?		D.	Mary and	Sue.

12   Activity Workbook

doing	watching	I'm	we're	you
reading	sleeping	he's	they're	what
playing	eating	she's	are	what's
studying	cooking			

1. _____What_____ are you doing?

   I'm _____ English.

2. What's Carla _____?

   _____.

3. _____ Walter doing?

   _____.

4. _____ _____ Julie and David doing?

   _____ _____ the newspaper.

5. _____ _____ you and George doing?

   _____ TV.

6. _____ _____ you _____?

   _____ the piano.

7. _____ William doing?

   _____ dinner.

Activity Workbook 13

cooking	eating	playing	singing	studying	watching
drinking	listening	reading	sleeping	teaching	

1. He's _____eating_____ breakfast.

2. She's _____ milk.

3. They're _____ mathematics.

4. He's _____ the newspaper.

5. They're _____.

6. She's _____.

7. He's _____ to music.

8. They're _____ TV.

9. She's _____ dinner.

10. He's _____.

11. They're _____ baseball.

Listen and put a check (✓) under the correct picture.

1. ___✔___   _____   2. _____   _____

3. _____   _____   4. _____   _____

5. _____   _____   6. _____   _____

7. _____   _____   8. _____   _____

9. _____   _____   10. _____   _____

D **GRAMMARRAP:** *Frank?! At the Bank?!*

Listen. Then clap and practice.

A. Where's Frank?

B. He's working at the bank.

A. Frank?! At the bank?!

B. Yes, that's right.
He's working at the bank.

All. Frank?! At the bank?! Oh, no!

A. Where's Sue?

B. She's working at the zoo.

A. Sue?! At the zoo?!

B. Yes, that's right.
She's working at the zoo.

All. Sue?! At the zoo?! Oh, no!

A. Where's Paul?

B. He's working at the mall.

A. Paul?! At the mall?!

B. Yes, that's right.
He's working at the mall.

All. Paul?! At the mall?! Oh, no!

WHAT'S THE QUESTION?

Where is	{ he she it } ?	What's	{ he she it } doing?
Where are	{ you they } ?	What are	{ you they } doing?

1. _Where_ _are_ _you_ ?

2. _What's_ _he_ _doing_ ?

3. _____ _____ _____ ?

4. _____ _____ _____ _____ ?

5. _____ _____ ?

6. _____ _____ _____ ?

7. _____ _____ _____ ?

8. _____ _____ _____ ?

9. _____ _____ _____ ?

10. _____ _____ ?

11. _____ _____ _____ _____ ?

12. _____ _____ _____ ?

I'm in the garage

He's cooking dinner.

They're in the park.

We're playing with the dog.

He's in the attic.

She's listening to the radio.

She's in the yard.

We're at the beach.

He's sleeping.

It's in the classroom.

They're eating lunch.

I'm in the hospital.

F **GRAMMARRAP:** *Eating Lunch*

Listen. Then clap and practice.

What's he	Where are	What are

A. Where's   Charlie?

B.   He's in the   kitchen.

A. What's he   doing?

B.   Eating   lunch.

All. Charlie's in the   kitchen   eating   lunch.

Charlie's in the   kitchen   eating   lunch.

A. Who's in the   kitchen?

B. Charlie's in the   kitchen.

A. What's he   doing?

B.   Eating   lunch.

A. Where's   Betty?

B.   She's in the   bedroom.

A. What's she   doing?

B.   Reading a   book.

All.	Betty's in the	bedroom	reading a	book.
	Betty's in the	bedroom	reading a	book.
A.	Who's in the	bedroom?		
B.	Betty's in the	bedroom.		
A.	What's she	doing?		
B.	Reading a	book.		

A.	Where are Mom and	Dad?
B.	They're in the	living room.
A.	What are they	doing?
B.	Watching Channel	Seven.

All.	Betty's in the	bedroom.
	Mom's in the	living room.
	Dad's in the	living room.
	Charlie's in the	kitchen.

A.	Where's	Charlie?
All.	He's in the	kitchen.
A.	What's he	doing?
All.	Eating	lunch.

✓ CHECK-UP TEST: Chapters 1-3

A. Answer the questions.

Ex. What's your telephone number?

My ___telephone number is 567-1032.___

1. What's your name?

....

2. What's your address?

....

3. Where are you from?

....

B. Circle the correct answer.

Ex. The map is on the
| yard |
| (wall) |
| park |

1. We're eating
| milk |
| cards |
| lunch |

2.
| What |
| Where's |
| What's |
Ben doing?

3. Max is
| planting flowers |
| swimming |
| singing |
in

the bathroom.

4. Ms. Park is teaching
| dinner |
| mathematics |
| the radio. |

5. Nice to
| hello |
| hi |
| meet |
you.

6. The
| pencil |
| attic |
| shower |
is in the classroom.

C. Fill in the blanks.

Ex. ___What's___ Bill doing?

1. Maria is _____ the hospital.

2. I'm _____ the newspaper.

3. Where's Joe? _____ in the cafeteria.

4. They're _____ TV.

5. What are you and Peter doing? _____
reading.

6. _____ the car? It's in the garage.

7. What are you _____? I'm
studying.

8. Where's the cell phone? _____
in the basement.

9. _____ are Mr. and Mrs. Chen doing?

10. Carol _____ Bob are eating
breakfast.

D. Listen and write the letter or number you hear.

Ex. M-A-R-_K_

1. C-A-R-___E-R

2. 354-9___12

3. 890-74___2

4. ___-U-L-I-E

5. 6___2-3059

6. 517___349

A WHAT ARE THEY DOING?

what	my	our	cleaning	apartment
what's	his	their	doing	children
are	her		fixing	homework
				sink

1. Hi! ___What's___ Jason doing?

   He's _____ _____ room.

2. What's Peggy _____?

   She's _____ _____ car.

3. _____ are you doing?

   I'm cleaning _____ _____.

4. What are your _____ doing?

   They're doing _____ _____.

5. What _____ you doing?

   We're fixing _____ _____.

Activity Workbook   **21**

B WHAT'S THE WORD?

my	his	her	its	our	your	their

1. I'm feeding ____my____ cat.

2. We're washing _____ clothes.

3. They're painting _____ bedroom.

4. She's fixing _____ sink.

5. It's eating _____ dinner.

6. You're cleaning _____ yard.

7. He's reading _____ e-mail.

C LISTENING

Listen and circle the word you hear.

1. your   (our)
2. his   her

3. her   his
4. our   their

5. your   our
6. my   its

D PUZZLE

Across

1. I'm painting _____ apartment.

3. We're fixing _____ TV.

6. Bobby and Tim are cleaning _____ room.

7. Bill is doing _____ homework.

Down

2. You're doing _____ exercises.

4. The dog is eating _____ dinner.

5. Ruth is brushing _____ teeth.

E WHAT ARE THEY SAYING?

| Yes, I am. | Yes, { he / she / it } is. | Yes, { we / you / they } are. |

1. A. Is Harry feeding his cat?

   B. __Yes,__ __he__ __is.__

2. A. Are you and Tom cleaning your yard?

   B. ___ ___ ___

3. A. Is Mrs. Chen doing her exercises?

   B. ___ ___ ___

4. A. Are your children brushing their teeth?

   B. ___ ___ ___

5. A. Is George sleeping?

   B. ___ ___ ___

6. A. Is Irene planting flowers?

   B. ___ ___ ___

7. A. Are you washing your windows?

   B. ___ ___ ___

8. A. Am I in the hospital?

   B. ___ ___ ___

Activity Workbook   **23**

Listen. Then clap and practice.

What are	Is he	Yes, he	What's he

A. Are you busy?

B.   Yes, I   am.

A.   What are you   doing?

B.   I'm talking to   Sam.

A.   Is he busy?

B.   Yes, he   is.

A.   What's he   doing?

B.   He's talking to   Liz.

A.   Are they busy?

B.   Yes, they   are.

A.   What are they   doing?

B.   They're washing their   car.

All.   I'm talking to   Sam.

He's talking to   Liz.

They're washing their   car.

They're busy!

G LISTENING

Listen and circle the word you hear.

1. (he's)   she's   3. feeding   eating   5. our   their

2. his   her   4. apartment yard   6. washing   watching

H WHAT ARE THEY DOING?

1. He's ____washing____ his hair.

2. They're _____ their yard.

3. We're _____ our exercises.

4. I'm _____ my e-mail.

5. She's _____ her living room.

6. You're _____ your cat.

I WHAT'S THE WORD?

Circle the correct words.

1. (They're) / Their washing they're / their windows.

2. Where / We're are Mr. and Mrs. Tanaka?

3. He's / His doing he's / his exercises.

4. Where are / Where's the cell phone?

5. We're brushing are / our teeth.

6. His / Is Richard busy?

7. What are / our you doing?

8. The cat is eating it's / its dinner.

Activity Workbook **25**

laundromat	doing	playing	they're	what's	her	are
library	eating	reading	he's	where's	their	and
park	fixing	washing	she's	in	his	
restaurant	listening					

Everybody is busy today. Ms. Roberts is in the ___restaurant___¹. She's _____²

dinner. Mr. and Mrs. Lopez are _____³ the health club. _____⁴ doing _____⁵

exercises. Patty and Danny Williams are in the _____⁶. She's _____⁷ the

newspaper. He's _____⁸ to music. Mr. _____⁹ Mrs. Sharp are also in the park.

What are they _____¹⁰? They're _____¹¹ cards.

Jenny Chang is in the _____¹². _____¹³ washing _____¹⁴ clothes.

Charlie Harris and Julie Carter _____¹⁵ in the parking lot. He's _____¹⁶

_____¹⁷ car. She's _____¹⁸ her bicycle. _____¹⁹ Mr. Molina? He's in the

_____²⁰. _____²¹ he doing? _____²² reading a book.

A MATCHING OPPOSITES

_d_	1.	large	a.	thin	___	8.	tall	h.	heavy

_d_ 1. large   a. thin   ___ 8. tall   h. heavy

___ 2. heavy   b. rich   ___ 9. difficult   i. old

___ 3. single   c. beautiful   ___ 10. new   j. ugly

___ 4. ugly   d. small   ___ 11. handsome k. big

___ 5. cheap   e. young   ___ 12. thin   l. easy

___ 6. poor   f. expensive   ___ 13. little   m. noisy

___ 7. old   g. married   ___ 14. quiet   n. short

B WHAT ARE THEY SAYING?

Tell me about your new friend.

1. Is he short or _____ tall _____?

2. Is he heavy or _____?

3. Is he old or _____?

4. Is he single or _____?

Tell me about the apartment.

5. Is it large or _____?

6. Is it quiet or _____?

7. Is it cheap or _____?

8. Is it beautiful or _____?

C LISTENING

Listen and circle the word you hear.

1. small   (tall)   3. easy   noisy   5. ugly   young

2. ugly   heavy   4. thin   single   6. cheap   easy

D WHAT'S WRONG?

He		
She }	isn't	They aren't
It		

1. It's new.

_____It isn't new._____

_____It's old._____

2. They're quiet.

_____

_____

3. It's large.

_____

_____

4. He's single.

_____

_____

5. She's young.

_____

_____

6. They're short.

_____

_____

E SCRAMBLED QUESTIONS

Unscramble the questions. Begin each question with a capital letter.

1. _____Are you busy_____?
   busy   you   are

2. _____?
   dog   your   large   is

3. _____?
   they   are   married

4. _____?
   I   beautiful   am

5. _____?
   difficult   English   is

6. _____?
   new   is   car   their

7. _____?
   tall   she   is   short   or

8. _____?
   noisy   quiet   he   is   or

F GRAMMARRAP: *Old! Cold! Tall! Small!*

Listen. Then clap and practice.

All.	Is he	young?	*(clap) (clap)*
	Is he	old?	*(clap) (clap)*
	Is it	hot?	*(clap) (clap)*
	Is it	cold?	*(clap) (clap)*
	Is she	short?	*(clap) (clap)*
	Is she	tall?	*(clap) (clap)*
	Is it	large?	*(clap) (clap)*
	Is it	small?	*(clap) (clap)*

Young!	Old!
Hot!	Cold!
Young!	Old!
Hot!	Cold!

A. Is he young or old?

B. He's very old.

A. Is it hot or cold?

B. It's very cold.

A. Is she short or tall?

B. She's very tall.

A. Is it large or small?

B. It's extremely small.

All. Young! Old!

Hot! Cold!

Short! Tall!

Large! Small!

Activity Workbook **29**

G WHOSE THINGS?

bicycle	book	car	cat	computer	dog	guitar	house	piano	TV

1. ___Albert's___ ___car___

2. _____ _____

3. _____ _____

4. _____ _____

5. _____ _____

6. _____ _____

7. _____ _____

8. _____ _____

9. _____ _____

10. _____ _____

H WHAT'S THE WORD?

His	Her	Their	Its

1. Mary's brother isn't short.   (His (Her)) brother is tall.
2. Mr. and Mrs. Miller's apartment isn't cheap.   (His   Their) apartment is expensive.
3. Robert's sister isn't single.   (His   Her) sister is married.
4. Ms. Clark's neighbors aren't quiet.   (Their   Her) neighbors are noisy.
5. Their dog's name isn't Rover.   (Its   Their) name is Fido.
6. Mrs. Hunter's car isn't large.   (His   Her) car is small.
7. Timmy's bicycle isn't new.   (His   Its) bicycle is old.
8. Mr. and Mrs. Lee's son isn't single.   (Her   Their) son is married.

I MR. AND MRS. GRANT

Read the story and answer the questions.

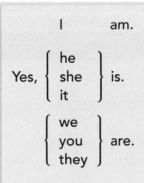

Yes,	I	am.
	he / she / it	is.
	we / you / they	are.

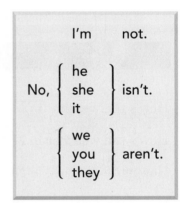

	I'm	not.
No,	he / she / it	isn't.
	we / you / they	aren't.

Meet Mr. and Mrs. Grant. Mr. Grant is short and heavy. Mrs. Grant is tall and thin. Their house is small and old. Their car is new and expensive. Their neighbors are noisy. And their cat is ugly.

1. Is Mr. Grant short? ___Yes, he is.___   8. Is their house large? _____
2. Is he tall? _____   9. Is it old? _____
3. Is he thin? _____   10. Is their car new? _____
4. Is he heavy? _____   11. Is it cheap? _____
5. Is Mrs. Grant tall? _____   12. Are their neighbors quiet? _____
6. Is she heavy? _____   13. Are they noisy? _____
7. Is she thin? _____   14. Is their cat pretty? _____

Activity Workbook   31

| it's sunny | it's raining | it's warm | it's hot |
| it's cloudy | it's snowing | it's cool | it's cold |

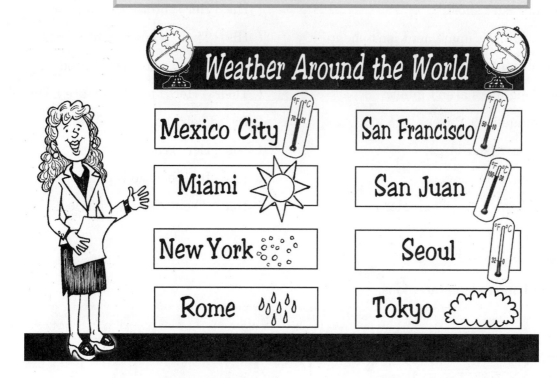

Weather Around the World

Mexico City
Miami
New York
Rome
San Francisco
San Juan
Seoul
Tokyo

1. How's the weather in Mexico City?   It's _____ warm.

2. How's the weather in Miami?   _____ _____

3. How's the weather in New York?   _____ _____

4. How's the weather in Rome?   _____ _____

5. How's the weather in San Francisco?   _____ _____

6. How's the weather in San Juan?   _____ _____

7. How's the weather in Seoul?   _____ _____

8. How's the weather in Tokyo?   _____ _____

9. How's the weather in YOUR city?   ....

K LISTENING

Listen and circle the word you hear.

1. cold   (cool)   3. sunny   snowing   5. raining   snowing

2. snowing   sunny   4. cool   hot   6. sunny   cloudy

Numbers

0	zero	10	ten	20	twenty	30	thirty
1	one	11	eleven	21	twenty-one	40	forty
2	two	12	twelve	22	twenty-two	50	fifty
3	three	13	thirteen	23	twenty-three	60	sixty
4	four	14	fourteen	24	twenty-four	70	seventy
5	five	15	fifteen	25	twenty-five	80	eighty
6	six	16	sixteen	26	twenty-six	90	ninety
7	seven	17	seventeen	27	twenty-seven	100	one hundred
8	eight	18	eighteen	28	twenty-eight		
9	nine	19	nineteen	29	twenty-nine		

L WHAT'S THE NUMBER?

1. twenty-four   24
2. thirty-one
3. seventy-two
4. forty-six
5. ninety-seven

M WHAT'S THE WORD?

38   thirty-eight
83
55
99
64

N NUMBER PUZZLE

Across

2. 46
5. 29
8. 8
9. 0
10. 11
11. 50

Down

1. 60
3. 15
4. 7
5. 20
6. 12
7. 90

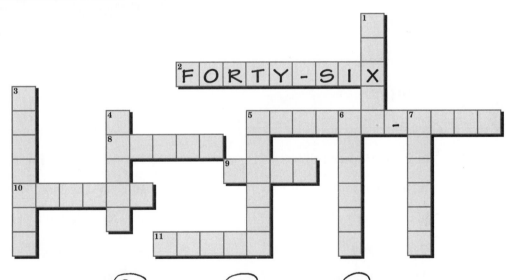

O LISTENING

Listen to the temperature in Fahrenheit and Celsius. Write the numbers you hear.

1. Los Angeles   _86°_ F/ _30°_ C
2. Seoul   _____ F/ _____ C
3. San Juan   _____ F/ _____ C
4. Hong Kong   _____ F/ _____ C

5. Miami   _____ F/ _____ C
6. London   _____ F/ _____ C
7. Mexico City   _____ F/ _____ C
8. Moscow   _____ F/ _____ C

P GRAMMARRAP: *Terrible Weather! Beautiful Weather!*

Listen. Then clap and practice.

It's raining in   Alaska.

It's snowing in   L.A.

It's cloudy in   Caracas.

It's TERRIBLE   today!

It's warm in   Pennsylvania.

It's sunny in   Bombay.

It's cool in   Guatemala.

It's BEAUTIFUL   today!

Q MATCHING

Match the questions and answers.

_e_ 1. Is your brother tall?

____ 2. Is your computer new?

____ 3. Is it hot today?

____ 4. Hi! Are you busy?

____ 5. Are your neighbors quiet?

____ 6. Is she young?

____ 7. Is her husband heavy?

____ 8. Is your sister married?

____ 9. Are these questions difficult?

a. Yes, I am. I'm studying.

b. No, she isn't. She's single.

c. No, she isn't. She's old.

d. No, it isn't. It's cold.

e. No, he isn't. He's short.

f. No, he isn't. He's thin.

g. No, they aren't. They're easy.

h. No, it isn't. It's old.

i. No, they aren't. They're noisy.

6

brother	sister
children	son
daughter	wife
husband	

father	grandmother
grandchildren	grandparents
granddaughter	grandson
grandfather	mother

Bill and Jane are married. Jane is Bill's ____wife____ 1. Bill is Jane's _____ 2.

Timmy and Sally are their _____ 3. Timmy is their _____ 4, and Sally is their

_____ 5. Timmy is Sally's _____ 6, and Sally is Timmy's _____ 7.

Walter and Helen are Jane's parents. Walter is Jane's _____ 8, and Helen is Jane's

_____ 9. Walter and Helen are Timmy and Sally's _____ 10. Walter is

their _____ 11, and Helen is their _____ 12. Timmy and Sally are

Walter and Helen's _____ 13. Timmy is their _____ 14, and Sally

is their _____ 15.

aunt	nephew	uncle
cousin	niece	

John is Jane's brother. Judy is John's wife.

Danny is their son. John is Timmy and Sally's

_____ 16, and Judy is their _____ 17.

Timmy is John and Judy's _____ 18,

and Sally is their _____ 19. Danny is

Timmy and Sally's _____ 20.

B LISTENING

Listen and put a check (✓) under the correct picture.

1. ___✓___ _____   2. _____   _____

3. _____   _____   4. _____   _____

5. _____   _____   6. _____   _____

7. _____   _____   8. _____   _____

C THE WRONG WORD!

Put a circle around the wrong word.

1.	large	small	(cheap)	little	6.	rugs	parents	cousins	children
2.	kitchen	bathroom	bedroom	park	7.	pencil	book	pen	bank
3.	guitar	baseball	drums	piano	8.	Miss	Mr.	Ms.	Mrs.
4.	handsome	beautiful	tall	pretty	9.	quiet	noisy	poor	loud
5.	hot	dinner	warm	cool	10.	son	sister	nephew	brother

Listen and fill in the words to the song. Then listen again and sing along.

crying	dancing	hanging	having	living	looking	smiling	working

I'm looking at the photographs.

They're hanging in the hall.

I'm ____smiling____ ¹ at the memories,

looking at the pictures on the wall.

My son Robert's married now.

I'm _____ ² in L.A. (Hi, Dad!)

My daughter's _____ ³ in Detroit.

I'm very far away. (I love you, Dad!)

I'm _____ ⁴ at the photographs.

They're _____ ⁵ in the hall.

I'm smiling at the memories,

looking at the pictures on the wall.

My mom and dad are _____ ⁶.

It's a very special day.

(We're _____ ⁷ a good time!)

My little sister's _____ ⁸.

It's my brother's wedding day.
(I'm so happy!)

I'm _____ ⁹ at the photographs.

They're _____ ¹⁰ in the hall.

I'm _____ ¹¹ at the memories,

_____ ¹² at the pictures on the wall.

I'm smiling at the memories,

looking at the pictures on the wall.

AN E-MAIL FROM LOS ANGELES

```
To: alex@ttm.com
From: bob@aal.com

Dear Alex,

    Our new home in Los Angeles is large and pretty.  Los Angeles is
beautiful.  The weather is warm and sunny.  Today it's 78˚F.
    Our family is in the park today, and we're having a good time.  My
mother is reading a book, and my father is listening to music.  My sister
Patty is riding her bicycle, and my brother Tom is skateboarding.
    My grandparents aren't in the park today.  They're at home.  My
grandmother is baking, and my grandfather is planting flowers
in the yard.
    How's  the weather in New York today?  Is it snowing?  What are
you and your family doing?
```

Answer these questions in complete sentences.

1. Where is Bob's new home? _____ It's in Los Angeles. _____

2. How's the weather in Los Angeles? _____

3. What's the temperature? _____

4. Where are Bob and his family today? _____

5. What's Bob's mother doing? _____

6. What's his father doing? _____

7. Who is Patty? _____

8. What's she doing? _____

9. Who is Tom? _____

10. What's he doing? _____

11. Are Bob's grandparents in the park? _____

12. Where are they? _____

13. What's his grandmother doing? _____

14. What's his grandfather doing? _____

15. Is Alex in Los Angeles? _____

16. Where is he? _____

Listen. Then clap and practice.

A.   What's Jack   doing?

B.   He's working in   Rome.

A.   What's BOB   doing?

B.   He's working at   HOME.

A.   Is Jack at   home?

B.   No. HE'S in   ROME.

A.   Is BOB in   Rome?

B.   No. HE'S at   HOME.

All.   Jack's in   Rome.

      Jack's in   Rome.

  What's BOB   doing?

    He's working at   HOME.

A.   What's Jane   doing?

B.   She's working in   Spain.

A.   What's MARY   doing?

B.   She's working in   MAINE.

A.   Is Jane in   Maine?

B.   No. SHE'S in   SPAIN.

A.   Is Mary in   Spain?

B.   No. SHE'S in   MAINE.

All.   Jane's in   Spain.

      Jane's in   Spain.

  What's MARY   doing?

    She's working in   MAINE.

✓ CHECK-UP TEST: Chapters 4-6

A. Circle the correct answers.

Ex. Jack is sitting on his **computer / TV / (bicycle)** .

1. He's my **nephew / wife / sister** .

2. We're standing **on / at / in** front of our house.

3. They're swimming at the **yard / kitchen / beach** .

4. He's feeding the dog **its / it's / he** dinner.

5. He's sleeping **at / on / in** the sofa.

6. Mrs. Kent is **raining / feeding / reading** in the park.

7. We're **fixing / snowing / riding** our car.

8. They're **painting / eating / brushing** their teeth.

B. Fill in the blanks.

Ex. ___What's___ his name?

1. _____ are they? They're in Tahiti.

2. My mother's mother is my _____.

3. My sister's daughter is my _____.

4. _____ is he? He's my cousin.

5. Mr. Jones is playing a game on _____ computer.

6. My children are doing _____ homework.

7. Ms. Kim is busy. She's fixing _____ sink.

C. Write a sentence with the opposite adjective.

Ex. Their car isn't cheap. ___It's expensive.___

1. My brother isn't heavy. _____

2. They aren't short. _____

3. My computer isn't old. _____

D. Write the question.

Ex. ___Is it ugly?___ No, it isn't. It's beautiful.

1. _____ No, I'm not. I'm single.

2. _____ No, she isn't. She's old.

3. _____ No, they aren't. They're noisy.

E. Listen and choose the correct response.

Ex. No, he isn't. (a.) He's young.   b. He's thin.

1. No, it isn't.   a. It's difficult. b. It's small.
2. No, she isn't. a. She's rich.   b. She's short.
3. No, it isn't.   a. It's easy.   b. It's cloudy.
4. No, he isn't.   a. He's tall.   b. He's loud.

WHERE IS IT?

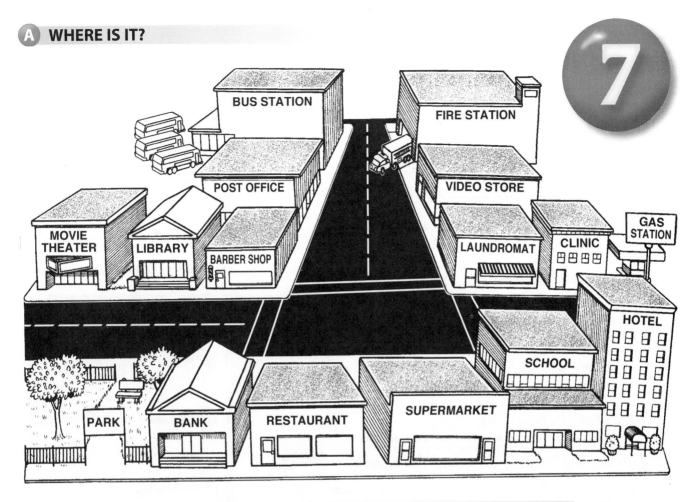

across from	around the corner from	next to	between

1. The bank is _____<u>next to</u>_____ the restaurant.

2. The bus station is _____ the fire station.

3. The library is _____ the movie theater and the barber shop.

4. The laundromat is _____ the video store.

5. The laundromat is _____ the clinic.

6. The clinic is _____ the laundromat and the gas station.

7. The clinic and the gas station are _____ the hotel.

8. The barber shop is _____ the post office.

9. The restaurant is _____ the supermarket.

10. The school is _____ the supermarket and the hotel.

11. The school is _____ the laundromat.

Is there	There's	across from	around the corner from
there		between	next to

1. Excuse me. Is there a bank in this neighborhood?

   Yes, there is. __There's__ a bank on Park Street, __next to__ the school.

2. Excuse me. _____ a video store in this neighborhood?

   Yes, there is. _____ a video store on Main Street, _____ the clinic.

3. Excuse me. Is there a supermarket in this neighborhood?

   Yes, _____ is. _____ a supermarket on School Street, _____ the post office.

4. Excuse me. _____ a park in this neighborhood?

   Yes, there is. _____ a park on State Street, _____ the drug store and the library.

5. Excuse me. _____ a gas station in this neighborhood?

   Yes, _____ is. _____ a gas station on _____ Avenue, _____ the fire station.

Listen to the sentences about the buildings on the map. After each sentence, write the name on the correct building.

1.	bakery	4.	library	7.	hair salon	10.	park
2.	school	5.	hospital	8.	supermarket	11.	health club
3.	department store	6.	police station	9.	video store	12.	train station

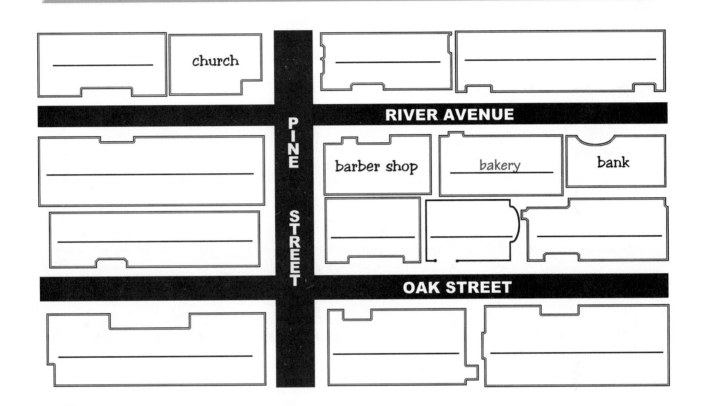

D **YES OR NO?**

Look at the map and answer the questions.

1. Is there a fire station on Oak Street?   Yes, there is.   No, there isn't.

2. Is there a hair salon across from the barber shop?   Yes, there is.   No, there isn't.

3. Is there a supermarket around the corner from the bank?   Yes, there is.   No, there isn't.

4. Is there a police station next to the hospital?   Yes, there is.   No, there isn't.

5. Is there a department store across from the school?   Yes, there is.   No, there isn't.

6. Is there a drug store on Oak Street?   Yes, there is.   No, there isn't.

7. Is there a laundromat next to the park?   Yes, there is.   No, there isn't.

8. Is there a church on River Avenue?   Yes, there is.   No, there isn't.

9. Is there a bank between the barber shop and the bakery?   Yes, there is.   No, there isn't.

Listen. Then clap and practice.

All. There's a nice big   supermarket   just around the   corner.

There's a good cheap   restaurant   just around the   corner.

There's a nice clean   laundromat   just around the   corner.

There's a quiet little   park   just around the   corner.

Just around the   corner?   Thanks   very much.

A. Is there a nice big   supermarket   anywhere   around here?

B. Yes, there   is.   Yes, there   is.

There's a nice big   supermarket   just around the   corner.

A. Just around the   corner?   Thanks very   much.

A. Is there a good cheap   restaurant   anywhere   around here?

B. Yes, there   is.   Yes, there   is.

There's a good cheap   restaurant   just around the   corner.

A. Just around the   corner?   Thanks very   much.

A. Is there a nice clean   laundromat   anywhere   around here?

B. Yes, there   is.   Yes, there   is.

There's a nice clean   laundromat   just around the   corner.

A. Just around the   corner?   Thanks very   much.

A. Is there a quiet little   park   anywhere   around here?

B. Yes, there   is.   Yes, there   is.

There's a quiet little   park   just around the   corner.

A. Just around the   corner?   Thanks very   much.

F WHAT ARE THEY SAYING?

is there	there is	there isn't	there are
are there	there's		there aren't

1. ____Is____ ____there____ an elevator in the building?

2. Yes, _____ _____.

3. How many closets _____ _____ in the apartment?

4. _____ a large closet in the bedroom, and _____ _____ two small closets in the living room.

5. _____ _____ a jacuzzi in the bathroom?

6. No, _____ _____. But _____ _____ two air conditioners in the apartment.

7. _____ _____ any washing machines in the building?

8. No, _____ _____. But _____ a laundromat across the street.

9. How many windows _____ _____ in the apartment?

10. _____ _____ three windows in the living room, and _____ one window in the bedroom.

G OUR APARTMENT BUILDING

broken	closets	escape	machines	satellite dish	mice
cats	dogs	hole	mailbox	refrigerator	stop

1. There aren't any washing _____machines_____ in the basement.

2. There's a _____ window in the bathroom.

3. There are _____ in the basement.

4. There isn't a fire _____.

5. There's a _____ in the wall in the living room.

6. There's a _____ on the roof.

7. There's a _____ in the kitchen.

8. There are two _____ in the bedroom.

9. There aren't any _____ in the building, but there are _____.

10. There isn't a bus _____ outside the building, but there's a _____.

| Yes, there is.   No, there isn't. | Yes, there are.   No, there aren't. |

1. Is there a computer in Jane's living room?

   _____ Yes, there is. _____

2. Is there a desk in the living room?

   _____

3. Are there any flowers in the living room?

   _____

4. Is there a newspaper on the table?

   _____

5. Are there any photographs on the table?

   _____

6. Are there any clothes in the closet?

   _____

7. Are there any windows in the living room?

   _____

8. Is there a cat in the living room?

   _____

9. Are there any chairs in front of the windows?

   _____

10. Is there a bookshelf in the living room?

    _____

11. Is there a cell phone next to the computer?

    _____

12. Is there a television next to the bookshelf?

    _____

13. Are there any books on the sofa?

    _____

14. Is there a guitar on the chair?

    _____

❶ LOOKING FOR AN APARTMENT

a/c. = air conditioner	beaut. = beautiful	frpl(s). = fireplace(s)	nr. = near
apt. = apartment	bldg. = building	kit. = kitchen	rm(s). = room(s)
bath(s). = bathroom(s)	dinrm. = dining room	lge. = large	schl. = school
bdrm(s). = bedroom(s)	elev. = elevator	livrm. = living room	

www.UShomes.com **CHICAGO**

Quiet, sunny apt., kit., livrm., bdrm., bath., 2 frpls., no children, $900. 800-874-5555.

1. The apartment is in _____Chicago_____.

2. It's quiet and _____.

3. There's a kitchen, a living room, a _____, and a _____.

4. There are two _____ in the apartment.

5. There aren't any _____ in the building.

www.UShomes.com **MIAMI**

Beaut. new apt., kit., livrm., 3 bdrms., 2 baths., elev. in building., $1200. 800-874-5555.

6. The apartment is in _____.

7. It's _____ and new.

8. There are three _____ in the apartment.

9. There are _____ bathrooms.

10. There's an _____ in the building.

www.UShomes.com **NEW YORK**

Sunny, lge. apt., kit., livrm., bdrm., bath., 2 a/c., nr. schl. $1800. 800-874-5555.

11. The apartment is in _____.

12. It's sunny and _____.

13. There's a kitchen, a _____, a bedroom, and a bathroom.

14. There are two _____.

15. The apartment is near a _____.

www.UShomes.com **DALLAS**

Lge. quiet apt., kit., livrm., dinrm., 2 bdrms., 2 baths., elev. in bldg., nr. bus. $850. 800-874-5555.

16. The apartment is in _____.

17. It's large and _____.

18. There's a _____, a kitchen, and a living room.

19. There's an elevator in the _____.

20. The apartment is _____ a bus stop.

J **GRAMMARRAP:** *Tell Me About the Apartment*

Listen. Then clap and practice.

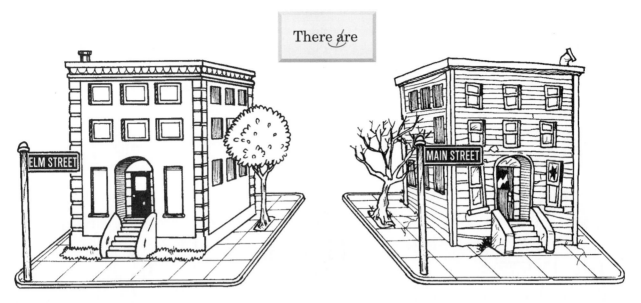

There are

A.	Tell me about the apartment on	Elm Street.	
B.	It's nice, but it	isn't very	cheap.
	There's a brand new	stove in the	kitchen.
	There's a beautiful	carpet on the	floor.
	There are three large	windows in the	living room.
	And the bedroom has a	sliding glass	door.
All.	The bedroom has a	sliding glass	door?!
B.	Yes, the bedroom has a	sliding glass	door.
A.	Tell me about the apartment on	Main Street.	
B.	It's cheap, but it	isn't very	nice.
	There isn't a	tub in the	bathroom.
	There aren't any	lights in the	hall.
	There's a broken	window in the	dining room.
	And there are ten big	holes in the	wall!
All.	There are ten big	holes in the	wall?!
B.	Yes, there are ten big	holes in the	wall.

belt	briefcase	glasses	jeans	purse	sock	tie
blouse	coat	glove	mitten	shirt	stocking	umbrella
boots	dress	hat	necklace	shoe	suit	watch
bracelet	earring	jacket	pants	skirt	sweater	

1. _____tie_____
2. _____
3. _____
4. _____
5. _____

6. _____
7. _____
8. _____
9. _____
10. _____

11. _____
12. _____
13. _____
14. _____
15. _____

16. _____
17. _____
18. _____
19. _____

20. _____
21. _____
22. _____
23. _____

24. _____
25. _____
26. _____
27. _____

B A OR AN ?

1. __a__ bus station
2. __an__ umbrella
3. _____ school
4. _____ office
5. _____ radio
6. _____ earring

7. _____ hospital
8. _____ antenna
9. _____ e-mail
10. _____ yard
11. _____ library
12. _____ cell phone

13. _____ exercise
14. _____ house
15. _____ bank
16. _____ woman
17. _____ apartment
18. _____ laundromat

19. _____ uncle
20. _____ attic
21. _____ flower
22. _____ aunt
23. _____ fax
24. _____ hotel

C SINGULAR/PLURAL

1. ___a hat___ hats
2. _____ basements
3. a dress _____
4. a boss _____
5. an exercise _____
6. _____ watches
7. _____ gloves
8. a sock _____
9. a drum _____

10. _____ rooms
11. an earring _____
12. _____ purses
13. a niece _____
14. a woman _____
15. _____ children
16. a mouse _____
17. _____ teeth
18. _____ people

D LISTENING

Listen and circle the word you hear.

1. umbrella   (umbrellas)
2. blouse   blouses
3. coat   coats
4. computer   computers
5. shoe   shoes
6. exercise   exercises
7. dress   dresses
8. restaurant restaurants

9. necklace   necklaces
10. earring   earrings
11. belt   belts
12. watch   watches
13. niece   nieces
14. nephew   nephews
15. shirt   shirts
16. tie   ties

E LISTENING

Listen and circle the color you hear.

1. (blue)   black   3. gray   gold   5. purple   yellow

2. red   green   4. pink   silver   6. orange   brown

F COLORS

Write sentences about yourself, using colors.

black	gray	pink	silver
blue	green	purple	white
brown	orange	red	yellow
gold			

1. My house/apartment is. . . . .

2. My bedroom is . . . .

3. My kitchen is . . . .

4. My bathroom is . . . .

5. My living room is . . . .

6. My classroom is . . . .

7. My English book is . . . .

8. My pencils are . . . .

9. My notebook is . . . .

10. My desk is . . . .

11. My shirt/blouse is. . . . .

12. My watch is . . . .

13. My socks/stockings are . . . .

14. My coat is . . . .

15. My hat is . . . .

16. My jeans are . . . .

17. My shoes are . . . .

18. My . . . . (is/are) . . . .

19. My . . . . (is/are) . . . .

20. My . . . . (is/are) . . . .

21. My . . . . (is/are) . . . .

22. My . . . . (is/are) . . . .

23. My . . . . (is/are) . . . .

24. My . . . . (is/are) . . . .

G WHAT ARE THEY LOOKING FOR?

1. Yes, please. I'm looking for

_____ a pair of pants _____ .

2. Yes, please. I'm looking for

_____ .

3. Yes, please. I'm looking for

_____ .

4. Yes, please. I'm looking for

_____ .

5. Yes, please. I'm looking for

_____ .

6. Yes, please. I'm looking for

_____ .

7. Yes, please. I'm looking for

_____ .

8. Yes, please. I'm looking for

_____ .

9. Yes, please. I'm looking for

_____ .

Listen and put a check (✓) under the correct picture.

1. _____   _____   2. _____   _____

3. _____   _____   4. _____   _____

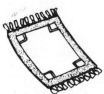
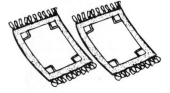

5. _____   _____   6. _____   _____

7. _____   _____   8. _____   _____

I **LISTENING**

Listen and circle the correct word to complete the sentence.

1. ⬭is⬭ are   red.   4. is / are   gold.   7. is / are   expensive.

2. is / are   easy.   5. is / are   beautiful.   8. is / are   small.

3. is / are   large.   6. is / are   new.   9. is / are   big.

J THIS /THAT /THESE /THOSE

 this these — that those

  orange

 yellow

1. _____This hat is orange._____

2. _____That hat is yellow._____

  brown

 black

3. _____

4. _____

  expensive

 cheap

5. _____

6. _____

  small

 large

7. _____

8. _____

  pretty

 ugly

9. _____

10. _____

  gold

 silver

11. _____

12. _____

K SINGULAR → PLURAL

Write the sentence in the plural.

1. That coat is blue.   _____Those coats are blue._____

2. This bracelet is new.   _____

3. That watch is beautiful.   _____

4. This is Tom's jacket.   _____

5. This isn't your shoe.   _____

6. Is that your earring?   _____

7. That isn't your notebook.   _____

8. This person isn't rich.   _____

L PLURAL → SINGULAR

Write the sentence in the singular.

1. These sweaters are pretty.   _____This sweater is pretty._____

2. Those purses are expensive.   _____

3. Are these your neighbors?   _____

4. Are those your dresses?   _____

5. Those are Bill's shirts.   _____

6. These women are my friends.   _____

7. These aren't my gloves.   _____

8. Those are her cats.   _____

M SCRAMBLED SENTENCES

Unscramble the sentences. Begin each sentence with a capital letter.

1. _____I think that's my jacket._____
   jacket I that's think my

2. _____
   my these gloves new are

3. _____
   boots aren't those black your

4. _____
   year blue very this suits popular are

5. _____
   of here's nice sunglasses pair a

6. _____
   old that's car brother's my

N GRAMMARRAP: *Clothes In My Closet*

Listen. Then clap and practice.

This shirt is	red.		Old	red	shirt!
That skirt is	blue.		New	blue	skirt!
This shirt is	old.		Old	red	shirt!
That skirt is	new.		New	blue	skirt!

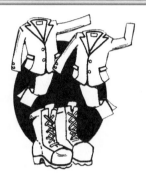

These suits are	silver.		New	silver	suits!
Those boots are	gold.		Old	gold	boots!
These suits are	new.		New	silver	suits!
Those boots are	old.		Old	gold	boots!

O GRAMMARRAP: *Black Leather Jacket*

Listen. Then clap and practice.

Blue	jeans,	gray	pants,
Black	leather	jacket!	
Blue	jeans,	gray	pants,
Black	leather	jacket!	

White	shirt,	silver	boots,
Black	leather	jacket!	
White	shirt,	silver	boots,
Black	leather	jacket!	

Cool	blue	jeans!	
Nice	gray	pants!	
White	shirt,	silver	boots,
Black	leather	jacket!	

this these		that those

1. _____This_____ is my favorite pair of jeans.

   _____ are my new sweaters, and

   _____ is my new coat.

2. _____That_____ 's a pretty coat.

   Are _____ your new boots?

3. _____ is my classroom.

   _____ is the bulletin board, and

   _____ are the computers.

4. Are _____ your books, and

   is _____ your pencil?

5. _____ is my favorite photograph.

   _____ is my mother, and

   _____ are my sisters and
   brothers.

6. Are _____ your cousins?

   Who's _____ handsome man?

Q GRAMMARSONG: *At the Laundromat*

Listen and fill in the words to the song. Then listen again and sing along.

hat	those	shirt	suits	that	are	skirt	that's	boots	these	this

Is ___this___ ¹ your sweater?

Is _____ ² your _____ ³?

_____ ⁴ my blue jacket.

That's my pink _____ ⁵.

I think _____ ⁶ is my new _____ ⁷.

We're looking for _____ ⁸ and _____ ⁹.

We're washing all our clothes at the laundromat.

_____ ¹⁰ and that. At the laundromat.

This and _____ ¹¹. At the laundromat.

_____ ¹² and _____ ¹³. At the laundromat.

Are _____ ¹⁴ your mittens?

_____ ¹⁵ these your _____ ¹⁶?

_____ ¹⁷ are my socks.

Those are my bathing _____ ¹⁸.

Where _____ ¹⁹ my pantyhose?

We're looking for _____ ²⁰ and _____ ²¹.

We're washing all our clothes at the laundromat.

_____ ²² and _____ ²³.

Washing all our clothes.

_____ ²⁴ and _____ ²⁵.

At the laundromat. At the laundromat.

(Hey! Give me _____ ²⁶!)

At the laundromat!

Activity Workbook   59 ●

✓ CHECK-UP TEST: Chapters 7-8

A. Circle the correct answers.

Ex. My favorite color is ~~broken~~ (blue) ~~big~~ .

1. Are ~~these~~ / **this** / ~~that~~ your children?

2. Here's a nice pair ~~to~~ / **on** / **of** stockings.

3. **Are there** / **Is there** / **There** a jacuzzi in the apartment?

4. There's an **earring** / **sweater** / **umbrellas** on the table.

5. **Who** / **What** / **How** many windows are there in the living room?

6. There aren't any **man** / **people** / **hole** in the room.

7. Dresses are over **there** / **their** / **they're** .

8. Is there a stove in the kitchen?

No, there aren't.
No, they isn't.
No, there isn't.

B. Answer the questions.

Ex. Where's the book store?

It's next to the bank.

1. Where's the bakery?

2. Where's the hospital?

_____

3. Where's the video store?

_____

C. Circle the word that doesn't belong.

Ex.	cotton	wool	vinyl	(cheap)
1.	this	those	their	these
2.	orange	striped	gray	pink
3.	closet	bakery	hotel	school
4.	boots	necklace	shoes	socks

D. Write sentences with *this*, *that*, *these*, and *those*.

old

Ex. _____ This car is old. _____

large

1. _____

broken

2. _____

black

3. _____

E. Write these sentences in the plural.

Ex. That house is large.

_____ Those houses are large. _____

1. This room is small.

_____

2. That isn't my pencil.

_____

3. Is this your boot?

_____

F. Listen and circle the correct word to complete the sentence.

Ex. is
(are) green.

1. is
are old.

2. is
are nice.

3. is
are beautiful.

4. is
are expensive.

INTERVIEWS AROUND THE WORLD

what	language	we	our	is	eat	read
what's	name	you	your	are	live	watch
where	names	they	their	do	sing	speak

A. _What's_ ¹ your name?

B. My _name_ ² _is_ ³ Sung Hee.

A. Where _do_ ⁴ _you_ ⁵ live?

B. I _live_ ⁶ in Seoul.

A. _What_ ⁷ _language_ ⁸ do you speak?

B. I _speak_ ⁹ Korean.

A. What _do_ ¹⁰ _you_ ¹¹ do every day?

B. Every day I _eat_ ¹² Korean food, and

I _watch_ ¹³ Korean TV shows.

A. What _are_ ¹⁴ your names?

B. _Our_ ¹⁵ _names_ ¹⁶ are Carlos and Maria.

A. Where _do_ ¹⁷ _you_ ¹⁸ live?

B. _We_ ¹⁹ _live_ ²⁰ in Madrid.

A. _What_ ²¹ language _do_ ²² _you_ ²³ speak?

B. We _speak_ ²⁴ Spanish.

A. What _do_ ²⁵ you _do_ ²⁶ every day?

B. Every day _we_ ²⁷ _sing_ ²⁸ Spanish songs,

and we _read_ ²⁹ Spanish newspapers.

A. <u>What</u> 30 <u>are</u> 31 their names?

B. <u>Their</u> 32 <u>names</u> 33 <u>are</u> 34
Yuko and Toshi.

A. <u>Where</u> 35 <u>do</u> 36 they live?

B. <u>they</u> 37 <u>live</u> 38 in Kyoto.

A. <u>what</u> 39 <u>language</u> 40 <u>do</u> 41
<u>they</u> 42 speak?

B. They <u>speak</u> 43 Japanese.

A. What <u>are</u> 44 they <u>do</u> 45 every day?

B. Every day <u>we</u> 46 <u>eat</u> 47 Japanese food,
and <u>we</u> 48 <u>watch</u> 49 Japanese TV shows.

B LISTENING

Listen and choose the correct response.

1. a. My name is Kenji.
    b. I live in Tokyo.

2. a. They speak Italian.
    b. I speak Italian.

3. a. They watch Russian TV shows.
    b. I watch Russian TV shows.

4. a. We live in Seoul.
    b. They live in Seoul.

5. a. We eat French food.
    b. We speak French.

6. a. They live in Madrid.
    b. We sing Spanish songs.

C PEOPLE AROUND THE WORLD

My name is Jane. I live in Montreal. Every day I play the piano, and I listen to Canadian music.

1. What's her name? _____ Her name is Jane.

2. Where does she live? <u>She lives in Montreal</u>

3. What does she do every day? <u>She plays the piano and she listen canadian Music.</u>

(continued)

My name is Omar. I live in Cairo. I speak Arabic. Every day I eat Egyptian food, and I read Egyptian newspapers.

4. What's his name _____? His name is Omar.

5. Where does he live _____? He lives in Cairo.

6. What language does he speak? He speaks Egyptian _____

7. What does he do _____ every day? He __eats__ Egyptian food, and He reads Egyptian newspapers _____.

My name is Sonia. I live in Sao Paolo. I speak Portuguese. Every day I do exercises, and I play soccer.

8. What's her name? Her name is Sonia

9. Where does _____ she live? She lives in Sao Paolo

10. What language __does she speak__? She speaks Portuguese

11. What __does she do__ every day? She does exercises, and she plays soccer.

D WRITE ABOUT YOURSELF

1. What's your name? My name is Enrique

2. Where do you live? I live in Plainfield

3. What language do you speak? I speak Spanish

4. What do you do every day? I work from 8 to 15 Am 3 Pm and then going home and watch some tv. and I write articles.

Listen. Then clap and practice.

A.   What's his   name?

B.   His name is   Joe.

A.   Where does he live?

B.   In Mexico.

A.   What's his   name?

B.   His name is   Lance.

A.   Where does he live?

B.   He lives in   France.

A.   What's her   name?

B.   Her name is   Anne.

A.   Where does she live?

B.   She lives in   Japan.

A.   What's her   name?

B.   Her name is Anastasia.

A.   Where does she live?

B.   She lives in   Malaysia.

A.   What's her   name?

B.   Her name is   Denise.

A.   Where does she live?

B.   She lives in   Greece.

A.   What's her   name?

B.   Her name is   Maria.

A.   Where does she live?

B.   She lives in   Korea.

Fill in the correct form of the verb.

clean	cook	do	live	play	read	shop	speak	work
cleans	cooks	does	lives	plays	reads	shops	speaks	works

My name is Eduardo. I ____live____ ¹ in Rio de Janeiro. I _____ ² English and

Portuguese. My wife's name is Sonia. She _____ ³ English, Portuguese, and Spanish. Our

children, Fernando and Claudio, also _____ ⁴ English and Portuguese. At school they

_____ ⁵ English and Portuguese books.

We _____ ⁶ in a large apartment. Every day my wife _____ ⁷ the newspaper

and _____ ⁸ in a bank. I _____ ⁹ breakfast and _____ ¹⁰ in an office.

Every weekend we _____ ¹¹ our apartment. I also _____ ¹² at the supermarket.

Fernando _____ ¹³ soccer with his friends, and Claudio and I _____ ¹⁴ basketball.

What languages _____ ¹⁵ YOU speak? What do YOU _____ ¹⁶ every day?

G **LISTENING**

Listen and circle the word you hear.

1.	(live)	lives	4.	listen	listens	7.	sing	sings
2.	do	does	5.	watch	watches	8.	eat	eats
3.	do	does	6.	eat	eats	9.	read	reads

do does	cook	drive	live	paint	sell

1. A. Where _____does_____ he live?

   B. He _____lives_____ in San Francisco.

2. A. What _____ they do?

   B. They _____ houses.

3. A. What _____ he do?

   B. He _____ a bus.

4. A. Where _____ you live?

   B. I _____ in Sydney.

5. A. What _____ you do?

   B. We _____ in a restaurant.

6. A. What _____ he _____?

   B. He _____ cars.

I **WHAT'S THE DIFFERENCE?**

1. I drive a bus. My friend Carla _____drives_____ a taxi.

2. We _____ in a bank. They work in an office.

3. Victor _____ the violin. His children play the piano.

4. I sell cars. My wife _____ computers.

5. I paint houses. My brother _____ pictures.

6. We live in Los Angeles. Our son _____ in London.

J LISTEN AND PRONOUNCE

Listen to each word and then say it.

1. chair
2. bench
3. Charlie
4. Chen
5. kitchen
6. Chinese
7. church
8. cheap
9. watch
10. children
11. Richard
12. shoes
13. Sharp
14. shirt
15. machine
16. Shirley
17. washing
18. station
19. short
20. English
21. French

K LOUD AND CLEAR Ch! Sh!

Fill in the words. Then read the sentences aloud.

chair	Charlie	kitchen	Chinese

1. ___Charlie___ is sitting in a ___chair___ in his ___kitchen___ and eating ___chinese___ food.

Shirley	short	shoes

2. ___Shirley___ isn't ___short___ in her new ___shoes___.

watch	Richard	cheap	French

3. ___Richard___ is looking for a ___cheap___ ___French___ ___watch___.

shirt	washing	washing machine

4. He's ___washing___ his ___shirt___ in his ___washing___ ___machine___.

bench	children	Chen	church

5. Mr. ___Chen___ and his ___children___ are sitting on a ___bench___ in front of the ___church___.

Sharp	station	English

6. Mr. ___Sharp___ is in London at an ___English___ train ___station___.

68 Activity Workbook

A WHAT'S THE DAY?

1. Monday ____Tuesday____ Wednesday
2. Friday ____Saturday____ Sunday
3. Tuesday ____Wednesday____Thursday
4. Saturday ____Sunday____ Monday
5. Thursday ____Friday____ Saturday
6. Sunday ____Monday____ Tuesday

B WHAT ARE THEY SAYING?

Yes, { he / she / it } does. No, { he / she / it } doesn't.

| what kind of |
| when |

1. ____Does____ your husband cook breakfast every day?

   Yes, ____he does____.

3. ____does____ your son drive a car?

   No, ____he doesn't____.

5. ____does____ that dog live in this neighborhood?

   No, it ____it doesn't____.

7. ____does____ your sister work at the bank?

   No, ____she doesn't____.

2. ____does____ your daughter study English in school?

   Yes, ____she does____.

4. ____what kind of____ food does he cook?

   He cooks Italian food.

6. ____does____ your grandfather shop at the grocery store in his neighborhood?

   Yes, ____he does____.

8. ____When____ does Robert visit his friends?

   He visits his friends on Sunday.

C WHAT ARE THEY SAYING?

Yes, { I / we / you / they } do.　　No, { I / we / you / they } don't.

1.

___Do___ you sing in the shower?

Yes, ___I do___.

2.

___do___ your children speak French?

No, ___they don't___.

3.

___do___ you and your husband live in this neighborhood?

Yes, ___we do___.

4.

___do___ you and your wife play cards?

No, ___we don't___.

5.

___do___ you work on Saturday?

No, ___We don't___.

6.

___do___ your neighbors make a lot of noise?

Yes, ___they do___.

D LISTENING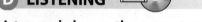

Listen and choose the correct response.

1. a. Chinese music.
   b. French food.
   c. Every day.

2. a. Yes, he does.
   b. No, we don't.
   c. Yes, they do.

3. a. No, he doesn't.
   b. Because he likes the food.
   c. On Wednesday.

4. a. On Sunday.
   b. Yes, she does.
   c. In her house.

5. a. I go every day.
   b. I don't go there.
   c. Yes, I do.

6. a. In New York.
   b. On Thursday.
   c. They don't go there.

7. a. Because it's open.
   b. They play.
   c. He rides his bicycle.

8. a. No, they don't.
   b. In the city.
   c. Yes, she does.

9. a. Because it's near their house.
   b. On Central Avenue.
   c. Yes, they do.

E YES AND NO

1. My husband cooks Italian food. He ___doesn't___ ___cook___ Thai food.

2. Linda drives a taxi. She ___doesn't___ ___drive___ a bus.

3. Our children play the piano. They ___don't___ ___play___ the guitar.

4. I work on Saturday. I ___don't___ ___work___ on Sunday.

5. Tom lives in an apartment. He ___doesn't___ ___live___ in a house.

6. My wife and I exercise in the park. We ___don't___ ___excercise___ in a health club.

7. Every Saturday Mrs. Roberts ___goes___ to the library. She doesn't go to the mall.

8. I ___shop___ in large supermarkets. I don't shop in small grocery stores.

9. My mother ___wears___ stockings. She doesn't wear socks.

10. Omar ___speaks___ Arabic. He doesn't speak Spanish.

11. Harry sings in the shower. He ___doesn't___ ___sing___ in the jacuzzi.

F WHAT'S THE WORD?

do	does

1. Where ___do___ they live?

2. When ___does___ your daughter do her homework?

3. What kind of books ___do___ you read?

4. Why ___does___ he call you every day?

5. What languages ___do___ they speak?

6. Where ___does___ your husband work?

7. ___do___ you visit your friends every week?

8. ___does___ he go to Stanley's Restaurant?

9. When ___do___ you go to the supermarket?

10. ___does___ your children wash the dishes?

11. What kind of music ___does___ she listen to?

12. What ___does___ he sell?

13. Why ___do___ they cry at weddings?

G WRITE ABOUT YOURSELF

1. I like ___blonds Girls___   I don't like ___Men___

2. I play ___baseball___   I don't play ___Golf.___

3. I speak ___Spanish and English___   I don't speak ___Russian___

4. I eat ___Mexican food___   I don't eat ___American Food___

5. I cook ___rarelly___   I don't cook ___every day___

YES OR NO?

1. Does Kathy take karate lessons?

   Yes, she does.

2. Do Jim and Tom play tennis on Sunday?

   No, they don't. They play volleyball.

3. Do you and Harry go dancing on Friday?

   yes ~~they~~ we do

4. Does Miguel play in the orchestra?

   No, ~~they don't.~~ he doesn't. he sings ~~They sing~~

5. Do you see a movie every weekend?

   no ~~I~~ don't

6. Do Mr. and Mrs. Kim go to a health club?

   Yes they do

7. Does Richard jog in the park?

   yes he does.

8. Do you and your wife watch TV every day?

   No we don't. We do yoga

LISTENING

Listen and choose the correct response.

1. a. Yes, they do.
   b. Yes, I do.

2. a. Yes, he does.
   b. Yes, I do.

3. a. No, he doesn't.
   b. No, they don't.

4. a. No, she doesn't.
   b. No, I don't.

5. a. Yes, we do.
   b. Yes, he does.

6. a. Yes, we do.
   b. No, they don't.

7. a. No, I don't.
   b. Yes, he does.

8. a. Yes, they do.
   b. Yes, he does.

9. a. No, we don't.
   b. No, they don't.

J **GRAMMARRAP:** *They Do, They Don't*

Listen. Then clap and practice.

Does he   Yes he   No he

A.   Does he eat French   bread?

B.   Yes, he   does.

A.   Does she like Swiss   cheese?

B.   Yes, she   does.

A.   Do they cook Greek   food?

B.   Yes, they   do.

A.   Do they speak   Chinese?

B.   Yes, they   do.

All.   He eats French   bread.

She likes Swiss   cheese.

They cook Greek   food.

And they speak   Chinese.

A.   Does he read the   paper?

B.   No, he   doesn't.

A.   Does she watch   TV?

B.   No, she   doesn't.

A.   Do they go to   movies?

B.   No, they   don't.

A.   Do they drink iced   tea?

B.   No, they   don't.

All.   He doesn't read the   paper.

She doesn't watch   TV.

They don't go to   movies.

And they don't drink   tea.

K A LETTER TO A PEN PAL

Read and practice.

Wednesday

Dear Peter,

My family and I live in San Juan. We speak Spanish. My mother is a music teacher. She plays the violin and the piano. My father works in an office.

My brother Ramon and I go to school every day. We study history, English, Spanish, science, and mathematics. My favorite school subject is science. I don't like history, but I like mathematics.

Do you like sports? Every day at school I play soccer. On Saturday I swim. What sports do you play? What kind of music do you like? I like rock music and country music very much, but I don't like jazz. What kind of movies do you like? I like adventure movies and comedies. I think science fiction movies are terrible.

Tell me about your family and your school.

Your friend,
Maria

L YOUR LETTER TO A PEN PAL

history
English
mathematics
science
music

---

baseball
football
hockey
golf
tennis
soccer

---

cartoons
dramas
comedies
westerns
adventure movies
science fiction
  movies

---

classical music
jazz
popular music
rock music
country music

Dear _Ana_,

My family and I live in _New Jersey_. We speak _English_. At school, I study _English_, _history_, and _mathematics_. My favorite subject is _science_. I don't like _history_.

What sports do you play? I play _baseball_ and _basketball_. I think _baseball_ is wonderful. I don't like _golf_.

What kind of movies do you like? I like _adventure movies_ and _science fiction_.

My favorite kind of music is _JAZZ_, and I like _classical music_. I don't listen to _popular music_.

Tell me about your school and your city.

Your friend,
Enrique

✓ CHECK-UP TEST: Chapters 9-10

A. Circle the correct answers.

Ex. We (live) / lives in Tokyo.

1. Tom play / (plays) in the park.

2. My wife and I (shop) / shops on Monday.

3. She don't / (doesn't) work on Saturday.

4. Where (do) / does your cousins live?

5. We stays / (stay) home every Sunday.

6. What activities do / (does) she do?

B. Fill in the blanks.

Ex. _____What_____ is your address?

1. _____Where_____ does he live?

2. _____What_____ kind of food do you like?

3. _____Why does_____ Patty baby-sit for her neighbors?

4. _____Why_____ do you eat at that restaurant?
   Because we like the food.

5. _____When_____ does Julie go to a health club?
   On Monday.

6. _____what_____ does your family do on Sunday?

C. Fill in the blanks.

Mrs. Davis _____lives_____¹ in Dallas. She's a very active person. She _____does_____² exercises every day. On Monday she _____cleans_____³ her apartment, on Wednesday she _____plays_____⁴ tennis, on Friday she _____takes_____⁵ a karate lesson, on Saturday she _____rides_____⁶ her bicycle in the park, and on Sunday she _____goes_____⁷ to a museum and eats _____(takes)_____⁸ lunch in a restaurant.

D. Listen and choose the correct response.

Ex. a. We go to school.
   (b.) They work in an office.
   c. They're shy.

1. a. Yes, we do.
   b. We like dramas.
   (c.) On Thursday.

2. a. In a restaurant.
   (b.) Because we like it.
   c. Every day.

3. a. Yes, they do.
   (b.) Yes, he does.
   c. In Puerto Rico.

4. (a.) Short stories.
   b. News programs.
   c. I like golf.

5. a. Yes, they do.
   b. Because it's convenient.
   (c.) On Center Street.

me	us
him	you
her	them
it	

1.

Do you like me?

Of course I like __you__.

2.

Do you like your neighbors?

Of course I like _____.

3.

Do you like Helen?

Of course I like _____.

4.

Do you like George?

Of course I like _____.

5.

Do you like videos?

Of course I like _____.

6.

Do you like English?

Of course I like _____.

7.

Do your friends like you?

Of course they like _____.

8.

Do you like your new apartment?

Of course I like _____.

9. Does your dog like you?

Of course he likes _____.

WHAT'S THE WORD?

it	her	him	them

1. She washes ___it___ every morning.

2. I think about _____ all the time.

3. We visit _____ every weekend.

4. I talk to _____ every night.

5. He uses _____ every day.

6. We feed _____ every afternoon.

C **LISTENING**

Listen and put a check (✓) under the correct picture.

1. _____ ___✔___

2. _____ _____

3. _____ _____

4. _____ _____

5. _____ _____

6. _____ _____

D **WRITE ABOUT YOURSELF**

1. I .... every day.

2. I .... every week.

3. I .... every month.

4. I .... every year.

5. I .... every weekend.

6. I .... every Sunday.

7. I .... every morning.

8. I .... all the time.

E. WRITE IT AND SAY IT

Write the correct form of the word in parentheses and then say the sentence.

1. Carol sometimes (eat) __eats__ Thai food.

2. My neighbor's dog always (bark) _____ in the afternoon.

3. My son never (clean) _____ his bedroom.

4. Ray always (wash) _____ his car on the weekend.

5. My brother sometimes (jog) _____ at night.

6. Amy usually (read) _____ poetry.

7. My mother rarely (shop) _____ at the grocery store around the corner.

8. Dan sometimes (watch) _____ videos on Saturday.

9. Omar usually (speak) _____ English at work.

10. Patty usually (play) _____ tennis in the park on Saturday.

F. MATCHING

__c__ 1. Walter always washes his car on Sunday.

_____ 2. Jonathan never cooks dinner.

_____ 3. Carla rarely watches comedies.

_____ 4. My grandmother rarely speaks English.

_____ 5. Richard usually jogs in the morning.

_____ 6. Larry never writes letters.

_____ 7. Nancy rarely studies at home.

_____ 8. Jane always fixes her computer.

a. She usually watches dramas.

b. He rarely jogs at night.

c. He never washes it during the week.

d. She usually studies in the library.

e. He always eats in a restaurant.

f. He always writes e-mail messages.

g. She usually speaks Spanish.

h. She never calls a repairperson.

G. LISTENING

Listen and choose the correct answer.

1. a. He usually washes it.
   b. He never washes it.

2. a. My husband sometimes cooks.
   b. My husband never cooks.

3. a. My neighbors are quiet.
   b. My neighbors are noisy.

4. a. They usually speak Spanish.
   b. They usually speak English.

5. a. Jane is shy.
   b. Jane is outgoing.

6. a. I usually study at home.
   b. I usually study in the library.

WRITE ABOUT YOURSELF

always	usually	sometimes	rarely	never

1. I _____ wear glasses.
2. I _____ eat Italian food.
3. I _____ listen to country music.
4. I _____ go to English class.
5. I _____ watch videos.
6. I _____ read poetry.
7. I _____ fix my car.
8. I _____ visit my grandparents.

9. I _____ watch game shows on TV.
10. I _____ use a cell phone.
11. I _____ clean my apartment.
12. I always _____ .
13. I usually _____ .
14. I sometimes _____ .
15. I rarely _____ .
16. I never _____ .

I **GRAMMARRAP:** *I Always Get to Work on Time*

Listen. Then clap and practice.

A. I always get to   work on time.

I'm usually here by   eight.

I sometimes get here   early.

I never get here   late.

No, I never get here   late.

B. He always gets to   work on time.

He's usually here by   eight.

He sometimes gets here early.

He rarely gets here   late.

A. No! I NEVER get here   late.

B. Right! He never gets here   late.

J WHAT'S THE WORD?

have	has

1. Do you ____have____ a bicycle?

2. My daughter _____ curly hair.

3. My parents _____ an old car.

4. Does your son _____ blond hair?

5. Our building _____ a satellite dish.

6. Do you _____ large sunglasses?

7. My sister _____ green eyes.

8. We _____ two dogs and a cat.

K WHAT ARE THEY SAYING?

have	has	do	does	don't	doesn't

1. ___Does___ your son ___have___ a bicycle?

   No. He ___doesn't___ ___have___ a bicycle. He __has__ a motorcycle.

2. Do you have short stories?

   No. We _____ short stories, but we _____ novels.

3. Do your children _____ a good teacher?

   Yes. They _____ a wonderful teacher.

4. What kind of computer _____ you _____?

   I _____ an IBM.

5. _____ they _____ jeans?

   No. They _____ _____ jeans, but they _____ jackets.

6. _____ this store _____ an elevator?

   No. It _____ _____ an elevator, but it _____ an escalator.

L WHAT'S THE WORD?

1. Tina doesn't have short hair. She has (long) / curly hair.

2. I don't have straight hair. I have thin / curly hair.

3. My brother isn't tall. He's heavy / short .

4. Albert isn't married. He's curly / single .

5. Your baby boy has beautiful blond eyes / hair .

6. His eyes aren't blue. They're brown / straight .

7. We don't live in the city. We live in the house / suburbs .

M TWO BROTHERS

My brother and I are very different. I'm tall, and he's __short__ ¹. I _____ ² brown eyes, and he _____ ³ blue eyes. We both _____ ⁴ brown hair, but I have long, straight hair, and he has _____ ⁵, _____ ⁶ hair. I'm short and heavy. And he's _____ ⁷ and _____ ⁸. I'm a chef, and _____ ⁹ a doctor. I live in New York. He _____ ¹⁰ in San Diego. I have a small apartment in the city. He _____ ¹¹ a large house _____ ¹² the suburbs. I play tennis. He _____ ¹³ golf. I play the guitar. He doesn't _____ ¹⁴ a musical instrument. On the weekend, I usually _____ ¹⁵ to parties. He doesn't _____ ¹⁶ to parties. He _____ ¹⁷ TV and _____ ¹⁸ the newspaper.

Listen and choose the correct response.

1. a. No. I have short hair.
    b. No. I have straight hair. *(b circled)*

2. a. No. I'm single.
    b. No. I'm tall and thin.

3. a. No. He has black eyes.
    b. No. He has brown eyes.

4. a. No. This is my mother.
    b. No. I have a sister.

5. a. Yes. I go to parties.
    b. Yes. I stay home.

6. a. Yes. He's thin.
    b. No. He's thin.

7. a. No. I live in an apartment.
    b. No. I live in the suburbs.

8. a. No. I have long hair.
    b. No. I have curly hair.

O WHAT'S THE WORD?

Circle the correct word.

1. He watches TV   at / with / **in** *(in circled)*   the evening.

2. The health club is   in / on / between   Main Street.

3. I'm playing a game   on / to / in   my computer.

4. Ann is sleeping   on / in / across   the yard.

5. He always talks   about / to / with   the weather.

6. I'm looking   from / for / to   a striped shirt.

7. Do you live   in / on / at   the suburbs?

8. Do your children go   to / at / in   school every day?

9. Tim is swimming   with / on / at   the beach.

10. My son is wearing a pair   from / for / of   new jeans.

11. Do you go   in / to / at   work   at / in / on   Saturday?

12. I listen   to / at / on   the radio in the morning.

WHAT'S THE WORD?

angry	embarrassed	hot	nervous	scared	thirsty
cold	happy	hungry	sad	sick	tired

1. Howard is crying. He's _____sad_____.

2. Helen is yawning. She's _____.

3. Sam is perspiring. He's _____.

4. Frank is shouting. He's _____.

5. Mrs. Allen is going to the hospital.

She's _____.

6. Peter is looking at his paper and smiling.

He's _____.

7. Ben's cat is eating. It's _____.

8. Irene is shivering. She's _____.

9. Louise is biting her nails.

She's _____.

10. Jason is covering his eyes.

He's _____.

11. Pam is drinking milk.

She's _____.

12. Bobby is blushing.

He's _____.

Activity Workbook**   **83**

1. A. Why are they yawning?

   B. <u>They're yawning because they're</u> tired.

   They always <u>yawn when they're tired</u>.

2. A. Why is she crying?

   B. _____ sad.

   She always _____.

3. A. Why is he shivering?

   B. _____ cold.

   He always _____.

4. A. Why are you perspiring?

   B. _____ hot.

   I always _____.

5. A. Why is she smiling?

   B. _____ happy.

   She always _____.

6. A. Why are they eating?

   B. _____ hungry.

   They always _____.

7. A. Why are you shouting?

   B. _____ angry.

   We always _____.

8. A. Why is he covering his eyes?

   B. _____ scared.

   He always _____.

Listen. Then clap and practice.

A.　　I smile when I'm　　happy.

I frown when I'm　　sad.

I blush when I'm　embarrassed.

And I shout when I'm　　mad.

B.　Are you smiling?

A.　Yes. I'm happy.

B.　Are you frowning?

A.　Yes. I'm sad.

B.　Are you blushing?

A.　　I'm embarrassed.

B.　Are you shouting?

A.　Yes. I'm mad.

D **GRAMMARRAP:** *Why Are You Doing That?*

Listen. Then clap and practice.

A.　　What's Fran　　doing?

B.　She's working　　late.

A.　　Working　　late?

Why's she doing　that?

B.　It's Monday.

She always works　late on　　Monday.

A.　　What are you　　doing?

B.　We're playing　　cards.

A.　　Playing　　cards?

Why are you doing that?

B.　It's Tuesday.

We always play　cards on　　Tuesday.

Activity Workbook　**85**

A. What's Bob doing?

B. He's cooking spaghetti.

A. Cooking spaghetti?

Why's he doing that?

B. It's Wednesday.

He always cooks spaghetti on Wednesday.

A. What's Maria doing?

B. She's dancing.

A. Dancing?

Why's she doing that?

B. It's Thursday.

She always dances on Thursday.

A. What's Gary doing?

B. He's bathing his cat.

A. Bathing his cat?

Why's he doing that?

B. It's Friday.

He always bathes his cat on Friday.

A. What are you doing?

B. I'm _____ing.

A. _____?

Why are you doing that?

B. It's Saturday.

I always _____ on Saturday.

1. A.   My sister is cooking dinner today.

    B.   That's strange! She never ___cooks___ dinner.

2. A.   Our children are studying with a flashlight.

    B.   That's strange! They never _____ with a flashlight.

3. A.   Victor is walking to work today.

    B.   That's strange! He never _____ to work.

4. A.   Ann is brushing her teeth in the kitchen.

    B.   That's strange! She never _____ her teeth in the kitchen.

5. A.   The dog is eating in the dining room today.
    B.   That's strange! It never _____ in the dining room.

6. A.   Nancy and Bob are dancing in the office.
    B.   That's strange! They never _____ in the office.

7. A.   Ruth _____ the carpet today.
    B.   That's strange! She never sweeps the carpet.

8. A.   My parents _____ poetry today.
    B.   That's strange! They never read poetry.

9. A.   _____ a typewriter today.

    B.   That's strange! You never use a typewriter.

10. A.   My cousins _____ in the yard.
    B.   That's strange! They never sleep in the yard.

F WHAT'S THE QUESTION?

Choose the correct question word. Then write the question.

What	When	Where	Why	What kind of	How many

1. I'm blushing <u>because I'm embarrassed</u>. _____ *Why are you blushing?* _____

2. They play tennis <u>in the park</u>. _____

3. She reads her e-mail <u>at night</u>. _____

4. I like <u>Brazilian</u> food. _____

5. We have <u>ten</u> cats. _____

6. He's using his <u>cell phone</u>. _____

What	How often	Where	Why	What kind of	How many

7. He watches <u>game</u> shows. _____

8. We call our grandchildren <u>every week</u>. _____

9. They <u>play golf</u> every weekend. _____

10. I'm smiling <u>because I'm happy</u>. _____

11. She's eating <u>in the cafeteria</u> today. _____

12. I'm wearing <u>two</u> sweaters. _____

G WHICH ONE DOESN'T BELONG?

#				
1.	her	me	them	(we)
2.	noisy	usually	sometimes	rarely
3.	does	doesn't	has	don't
4.	angry	yoga	nervous	happy
5.	Wednesday	Why	What	When
6.	smiling	shivering	crying	outgoing
7.	clean	sweep	shy	wash
8.	year	evening	night	afternoon

LISTENING

As you listen to each story, read the sentences and check *yes* or *no*.

Jennifer and Jason

1. yes ☐ no ☑ Jennifer and Jason are visiting their father.
2. yes ☐ no ☐ Jennifer and Jason are happy.
3. yes ☐ no ☐ Their grandfather isn't taking them to the park.

Our Boss

4. yes ☐ no ☐ Our boss usually smiles at the office.
5. yes ☐ no ☐ He's happy today.
6. yes ☐ no ☐ Everybody is thinking about the weekend.

On Vacation

7. yes ☐ no ☐ I like vacations.
8. yes ☐ no ☐ When the weather is nice, I watch videos.
9. yes ☐ no ☐ I'm swimming at the beach today because it's cold.

Timmy and His Brother

10. yes ☐ no ☐ Timmy is covering his eyes because he's sad.
11. yes ☐ no ☐ Timmy doesn't like science fiction movies.
12. yes ☐ no ☐ Timmy's brother is scared.

I **LOUD AND CLEAR** S! Z!

sorry hospital sick sister Sally

scientist speaking What's experiments

1. ___Sally___ is ___sorry___ her

   ___sister___ is ___sick___ in

   the ___hospital___ .

2. _____ the _____ doing?

   He's _____ about his new

   _____ .

always	cousin	Athens	busy	is

3. My _____ in _____

_____ _____ very

_____ .

doesn't	Sally's	clothes	husband	closet

4. _____ _____ _____

have any clean _____ in his

_____ .

Steven	it's	sweeping	is	because

5. _____ _____ _____

the floor _____ _____ dirty.

Sunday	Mrs.	newspaper	Garcia	reads

6. _____ _____ _____ the

_____ every _____ .

zoo	students	sometimes	bus	school

7. The _____ in our

_____ _____ go

to the _____ on the _____ .

plays	soccer	friends	Tuesday	son

8. My _____ Sam _____

_____ with his _____

every _____ .

✓ CHECK-UP TEST: Chapters 11–12

A. Fill in the blanks.

me	him	her	it	us	you	them

Ex. Do you like this book?
Of course I like ___it___.

1. Do you look like your father?
Yes. I look like _____.

2. When my cats are hungry, I always feed
_____.

3. Sally rarely plays with her sister, but she's
playing with _____ today.

4. I say "hello" to my boss every day, and he
says "hello" to _____.

5. We're going to the park. Do you want to go
with _____?

B. Fill in the blanks.

Ex. Betty never talks to her landlord, but
she's ___talking___ to him today.

1. We never feed the birds, but we're
_____ them today.

2. Harriet never _____ to parties, but
she's going to a party today.

3. My children never bake, but they're
_____ today.

4. Tim never _____ his TV, but he's
fixing it today.

5. Amy rarely _____ her kitchen
windows, but she's washing them today.

C. Fill in the blanks.

do	does	is	are

Ex. a. What __do__ you usually do on the
weekend?

b. What __is__ Tina doing today?

1. Why _____ the baby crying?

2. When _____ David and Pam go to the
supermarket?

3. _____ Bob usually dance?

4. Do they work here? Yes, they _____.

5. _____ your parents cooking lunch?

D. Write the question.

Ex. I'm shivering <u>because I'm cold</u>. (Why?)
<u>   Why are you shivering?   </u>

1. They work <u>in a laboratory</u> every day.
(Where?)
_____

2. We get together <u>on Saturday</u>. (When?)
_____

3. He's crying <u>because he's sad</u>. (Why?)
_____

4. She has <u>three</u> children. (How many?)
_____

5. I'm drinking <u>milk</u>. (What?)
_____

E. Listen and choose the correct response.

Ex. (a.) They're playing soccer.
b. They play tennis.

1. a. They're delivering mail.
b. They deliver mail.

2. a. We're going to the zoo.
b. We go to the park.

3. a. I'm covering my eyes.
b. I cover my eyes.

4. a. No, I don't.
b. No, I'm not.

5. a. I'm studying in the library.
b. I study in the library.

A CAN OR CAN'T?

cook	drive	play	skate	speak
dance	paint	sing	ski	use

1. Billy ___can't___ ___ski___.

   He ___can___ ___skate___.

2. Sally _____ _____.

   She _____ _____.

3. Edward _____ _____ pictures.

   He _____ _____ houses.

4. Carla _____ _____ Arabic.

   She _____ _____ Italian.

5. We _____ _____ Greek food.

   We _____ _____ Japanese food.

6. I _____ _____ a cash register.

   I _____ _____ a calculator.

7. They _____ _____ tennis.

   They _____ _____ baseball.

8. Harold _____ _____ a taxi.

   He _____ _____ a bus.

WHAT CAN YOU DO?

Check the things you can do. Then ask other students.

Can you . . .?	You		Student 1		Student 2	
1. cook	❏ yes	❏ no	❏ yes	❏ no	❏ yes	❏ no
2. swim	❏ yes	❏ no	❏ yes	❏ no	❏ yes	❏ no
3. ski	❏ yes	❏ no	❏ yes	❏ no	❏ yes	❏ no
4. skate	❏ yes	❏ no	❏ yes	❏ no	❏ yes	❏ no
5. paint	❏ yes	❏ no	❏ yes	❏ no	❏ yes	❏ no
6. drive	❏ yes	❏ no	❏ yes	❏ no	❏ yes	❏ no
7. play tennis	❏ yes	❏ no	❏ yes	❏ no	❏ yes	❏ no
8. speak Chinese	❏ yes	❏ no	❏ yes	❏ no	❏ yes	❏ no
9. use a cash register	❏ yes	❏ no	❏ yes	❏ no	❏ yes	❏ no

C **WHAT'S THE QUESTION?**

1. _____Can he cook_____?
Yes, he can.

2. _____?
No, she can't.

3. _____?
Yes, they can.

4. _____?
Yes, I can.

5. _____?
No, he can't.

6. _____?
No, we can't.

D **LISTENING**

Listen and circle the word you hear.

1. (can)	can't	4. can	can't	7. can	can't	10. can	can't
2. can	can't	5. can	can't	8. can	can't	11. can	can't
3. can	can't	6. can	can't	9. can	can't	12. can	can't

Activity Workbook 93

actor	actress	baker	chef	dancer	mechanic	secretary	singer	teacher	truck driver

Across

4. She fixes cars every day.
6. He teaches in a school.
7. She acts in the movies.
9. He dances every day.
10. He acts on TV.

Down

1. She drives a truck.
2. He types every day.
3. He cooks in a restaurant.
5. He bakes pies and cakes.
8. She sings on TV.

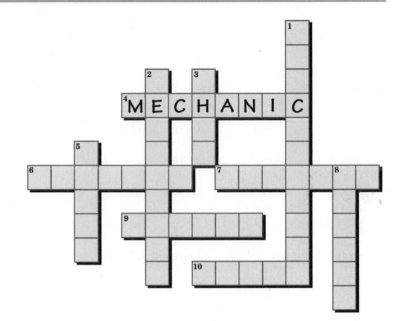

F *CAN OR CAN'T?*

1. My brother is a chef in a bakery. He ____can____ bake pies and cakes.

2. They ____can't____ sing. They aren't very good singers.

3. _____ Jane drive a truck? Of course she _____.
   She's a truck driver.

4. The chef in that restaurant _____ cook!
   The food is terrible!

5. Of course I _____ fix cars. I'm a mechanic.

6. That actor is terrible! He _____ act!

7. _____ they dance? Of course they _____.
   They're dancers on TV.

8. I'm a very good cashier. I _____ use a cash register.

9. My new secretary isn't very good. He _____ type, and he _____ speak on the telephone.

10. They're very athletic. They _____ skate, they _____ ski, and they _____ play soccer.

11. My friend George can only speak English. He _____ speak Spanish, and he _____ speak French.

G GRAMMARRAP: *Of Course They Can!*

Listen. Then clap and practice.

> She can speak.
> He can speak.
> We can speak.
> They can speak.

A.   Can Anne speak French?

B.   Of course she   can.

       She can speak French very   well.

A. Can the Browns play   tennis?

B.   Of course they   can.

       They can play   tennis very   well.

A.   Can Peter bake   pies?

B.   Of course he   can.

       He can bake   pies very   well.

A.   Can we speak   English?

B.   Of course we   can.

       We can speak   English very well.

H WHAT ARE THEY SAYING?

have to	do	don't
has to	does	doesn't

1. Can you play baseball with me?

   I'm sorry. I can't. I __have__ __to__ do my homework.

2. Why is Susie upset today?

   She _____ _____ go to the dentist this afternoon.

3. Can your husband fix the sink?

   No, he can't. He _____ _____ call a plumber.

4. Do I really _____ get a haircut?

   Yes, you do. You _____ get a haircut today.

5. _____ Grandma _____ _____ go to the doctor often?

   Yes, she _____. She _____ _____ go to the doctor every month.

6. _____ you _____ _____ work today?

   No, I _____. I'm on vacation.

7. Do you want to go skiing this weekend?

   This weekend? Sorry. We can't. We _____ _____ clean our apartment.

8. Are you bored?

   No. I'm tired. I _____ _____ go to bed.

I A BUSY FAMILY

Mr. and Mrs. Lane, their son Danny, and their daughter Julie are very busy this week.

Monday: Dad – speak to the superintendent
            Mom – meet with Danny's teacher
Tuesday: Danny and Julie – go to the doctor
Wednesday: Dad – fix the car

Thursday: Mom – go to the dentist
Friday: Julie – baby-sit
Saturday: Mom and Dad – clean the apartment
            Danny and Julie – plant flowers in the yard

1. What does Mr. Lane have to do on Monday? _____ He has to speak to the superintendent. _____

2. What does Mrs. Lane have to do on Monday? _____

3. What do Danny and Julie have to do on Tuesday? _____

4. What does Mr. Lane have to do on Wednesday? _____

5. What does Mrs. Lane have to do on Thursday? _____

6. What does Julie have to do on Friday? _____

7. What do Mr. and Mrs. Lane have to do on Saturday? _____

8. What do Danny and Julie have to do on Saturday? _____

J WRITE ABOUT YOURSELF

What do YOU have to do this week?

....

....

....

....

K LISTENING

Listen and circle the words you hear.

1. has to	(have to)	4. has to	have to	7. can	can't
2. has to	have to	5. can	can't	8. has to	have to
3. can	can't	6. has to	have to	9. can	can't

can't	baby-sit	go swimming	have dinner
have to	clean the house	go to a movie	study
has to	go bowling	go to a soccer game	wash my clothes
	go dancing	go to the dentist	work

1. I _____ can't go swimming _____
    today.

    I _____ have to go the dentist _____ .

2. Patty _____
    on Saturday.

    She _____ .

3. Bob and Julie _____
    today.

    They _____ .

4. Tom _____
    today.

    He _____ .

5. We _____
    on Saturday.

    We _____ .

6. I _____
    with you today.

    I _____ .

M **LISTENING**

Listen and choose the correct answer.

1. (a.) She has to go to the dentist.
    b. She can go to the movies.

2. a. He has to wash his car.
    b. He can't go to the party.

3. a. She can have lunch with her friend.
    b. She can have dinner with her friend.

4. a. They have to paint their kitchen.
    b. They can go skiing.

5. a. He has to cook lunch.
    b. He has to go shopping today.

6. a. She has to baby-sit on Friday.
    b. She can't see a play on Saturday.

N GRAMMARRAP: *Where Is Everybody?*

Listen. Then clap and practice.

A. Where's Joe?

B. He has to go.

A. Where's Ray?

B. He can't stay.

A. Where's Kate?

B. She can't wait.

A. Where's Steve?

B. He has to leave.

A. Where's Murray?

B. He has to hurry.

A. What about you?

B. I have to go, too.

All. Oh, no!

Joe has to go.

Ray can't stay.

Kate can't wait.

Steve has to leave.

Murray has to hurry.

What can I do?

I have to go, too.

O GRAMMARRAP: *Can't Talk Now*

Listen. Then clap and practice.

A. I can't talk now.

I have to go to work.

B. I can't stop now.

I have to catch a train.

C. I can't leave now.

I have to make a call.

D. I can't stop now.

I have to catch a plane.

All. She can't stop now.

She has to catch a train.

She can't stop now.

She has to catch a plane.

A WHAT ARE THEY GOING TO DO?

14

1. What's Larry going to do tomorrow?

   _____ He's going to cook. _____

2. What's Jane going to do tomorrow?

   _____

3. What are you going to do tomorrow?

   _____

4. What are they going to do tomorrow?

   _____

5. What are you and your friends going to do tomorrow?

   _____

6. What's William going to do tomorrow?

   _____

B WHAT ARE THEY SAYING?

1. ___ What are ___ you

   ___ going to do ___ tomorrow?

   ___ I'm going to ___ clean my apartment.

2. _____ your husband

   _____ tomorrow?

   _____ fix the kitchen sink.

3. _____ your mother

   _____ tomorrow?

   _____ plant flowers.

4. _____ your cousins

   _____ tomorrow?

   _____ visit us.

C WHAT ARE THEY GOING TO DO?

are	is	going	go	to

1. We're ___going___ ___to___ ___go___ dancing tonight.

2. They're ___going___ swimming this afternoon.

3. I'm _____ _____ _____ shopping tomorrow.

4. Brian _____ _____ _____ the library this morning.

5. Rita _____ _____ _____ _____ _____ a party tomorrow night.

6. My friends and I _____ _____ to a baseball game tomorrow afternoon.

7. Mr. and Mrs. Lopez _____ _____ _____ _____ _____ a concert this evening.

8. I'm _____ _____ the supermarket tomorrow morning, and my husband

   _____ _____ _____ _____ _____the bank.

D GRAMMARRAP: *What Are You Going to Do?*

Listen. Then clap and practice.

going to = gonna

All.	What are you going to do tomorrow	morning?	
	How about tomorrow	afternoon?	
	What are you going to do tomorrow	evening?	
	What are you going to do this	June?	
A.	I'm going to vacuum all my rugs tomorrow	morning.	
B.	I'm going to walk my dog tomorrow	afternoon.	
C.	I'm going to visit all my friends tomorrow	evening.	
D.	I'm going to dance at my wedding this	June.	

E WHICH WORD DOESN'T BELONG?

1. January	May	(Monday)	April
2. Tuesday	Saturday	Sunday	September
3. autumn	at once	winter	summer
4. Friday	February	March	October
5. him	them	he	her
6. right now	next week	at once	immediately

F WHAT'S NEXT?

1. June	July	<u>August</u>	
2. Monday	Tuesday	_____	
3. February	March	_____	

4. summer	fall	_____	
5. Friday	Saturday	_____	
6. October	November	_____	

G MATCH THE SENTENCES

Are you going to . . .

<u>c</u>   1. call your friends on Thursday?

_____   2. fix our doorbell this week?

_____   3. visit your aunt next summer?

_____   4. visit your cousins in April?

_____   5. fix our windows this month?

_____   6. call your uncle this June?

a. No. I'm going to visit them in October.

b. No. I'm going to visit her next winter.

c. No. I'm going to call them on Friday.

d. No. I'm going to fix them next month.

e. No. I'm going to call him this July.

f. No. I'm going to fix it next week.

H LISTENING

Listen and circle the words you hear.

1. (this)	next	5. Tuesday	Thursday	9. autumn	August
2. right now	right away	6. November	December	10. watch	wash
3. Monday	Sunday	7. spring	winter	11. next	this
4. wash	cut	8. at once	next month	12. number	plumber

I WHAT'S THE QUESTION?

1. We're going to <u>do our exercises</u> right now.   What _____<u>are you going to do right now?</u>_____

2. She's going to baby-sit <u>this Friday</u>.   When_____

3. We're going to <u>Paris</u> next April.   Where_____

4. I'm going to clean it <u>because it's dirty</u>.   Why_____

5. They're going to <u>go to the beach</u> today.   What_____

6. I'm going to fix the doorbell <u>next week</u>.   When_____

7. She's going to plant flowers <u>in her yard</u>.   Where_____

8. He's going to read his e-mail <u>right now</u>.   When_____

9. I'm going to bed now <u>because I'm tired</u>.   Why_____

J LISTENING

Listen to the following weather forecasts and circle the correct answers.

Today's Weather Forecast

| **This afternoon:** | hot | (cool) | sunny | (cloudy) |
| **This evening:** | foggy | clear | rain | warm |

This Weekend's Weather Forecast

Tonight:	cool	cold	clear	warm
Saturday:	cloudy	sunny	foggy	hot
Sunday:	foggy	cool	snow	rain

Monday's Weather Forecast

Monday morning:	cold	cool	cloudy	nice
Monday afternoon:	cool	cold	foggy	snow
Tuesday morning:	sunny	cloudy	nice	warm

K WHAT DOES EVERYBODY WANT TO DO TOMORROW?

want to	wants to

1. I ____want to____ have a picnic tomorrow.

2. George _____ work in his garden.

3. Karen _____ take her children to a concert.

4. Mr. and Mrs. Sato _____ go to the beach.

5. You _____ see a movie.

6. I _____ see a play.

7. My friends _____ go to a basketball game.

L BAD WEATHER

go skiing	go sailing	snow	be cold
take her son to the zoo	go jogging	rain	be warm

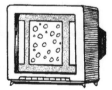

1. What does Richard want to do tomorrow?

_____He wants to go sailing._____

What's the forecast?

_____It's going to rain._____

2. What does Lucy want to do this afternoon?

_____

What's the forecast?

_____

3. What do Carl and Betty want to do today?

_____

What's the forecast?

_____

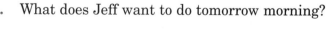

4. What does Jeff want to do tomorrow morning?

_____

What's the forecast?

_____

M YES AND NO

YES!

doesn't want to
don't want to

NO!

1. My parents want to buy a new car.

   <u>They don't want to buy</u> a motorcycle.

2. David wants to go to a baseball game.

   _____ to a concert.

3. I want to wash my car.

   _____ my clothes.

4. Nancy and Pam want to play baseball.

   _____ soccer.

5. Michael wants to cook Italian food.

   _____ American food.

6. We want to study English.

   _____ history.

7. Margaret wants to dance with John.

   _____ with Jim.

8. I want to work in the garden today.

   _____ in the kitchen.

N YES AND NO

I'm	not	
He She It	isn't	going to
We You They	aren't	

1. Steven is going to go swimming.

   <u>He isn't going to go</u> sailing.

2. I'm going to take a shower.

   _____ a bath.

3. We're going to go bowling.

   _____ shopping.

4. Barbara is going to go to the beach.

   _____ to the mall.

5. My parents are going to clean the attic.

   _____ the basement.

6. It's going to be warm.

   _____ cool.

7. Robert is going to listen to the news.

   _____ the forecast.

8. You're going to buy a used car.

   _____ a new car.

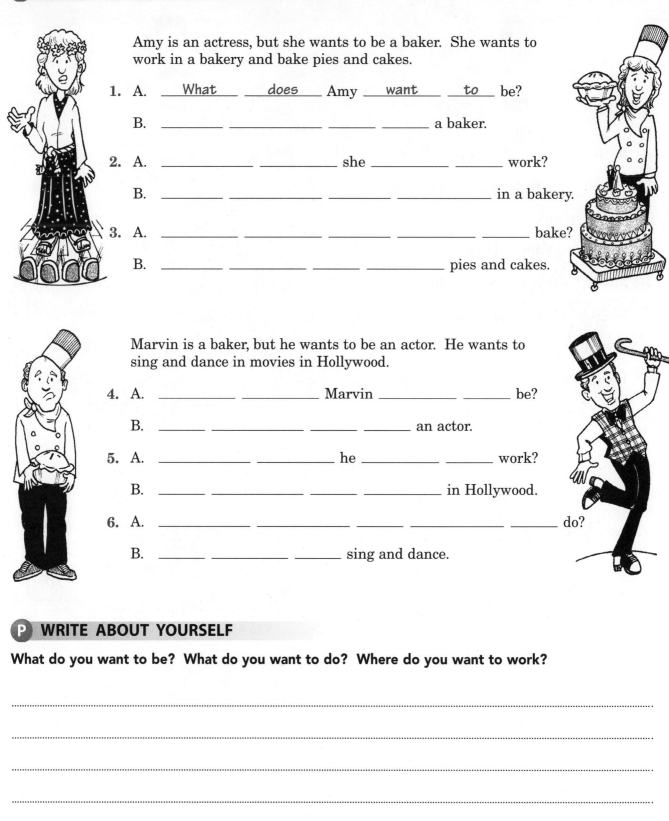

O WHAT DO THEY WANT TO BE?

Amy is an actress, but she wants to be a baker. She wants to work in a bakery and bake pies and cakes.

1. A. ___What___ ___does___ Amy ___want___ ___to___ be?

   B. _____ _____ _____ _____ a baker.

2. A. _____ _____ she _____ _____ work?

   B. _____ _____ _____ _____ in a bakery.

3. A. _____ _____ _____ _____ _____ bake?

   B. _____ _____ _____ _____ pies and cakes.

Marvin is a baker, but he wants to be an actor. He wants to sing and dance in movies in Hollywood.

4. A. _____ _____ Marvin _____ _____ be?

   B. _____ _____ _____ _____ an actor.

5. A. _____ _____ he _____ _____ work?

   B. _____ _____ _____ _____ in Hollywood.

6. A. _____ _____ _____ _____ _____ do?

   B. _____ _____ _____ sing and dance.

P WRITE ABOUT YOURSELF

What do you want to be? What do you want to do? Where do you want to work?

....

....

....

....

....

....

GRAMMARRAP: *What Do They Want to Do?*

Listen. Then clap and practice.

> want to = wanna
> wants to = wantsta

He wants to   go.
I want to   stay.
He wants to   work.
I want to   play.

She wants to   eat at a   restaurant.
I want to   eat at   home.
She wants to   eat with   all our   friends.
I want to   eat   alone.

We want to   leave at   seven.
They want to   leave at   eight.
We want to   get there   early.
They want to   get there   late.

Jack wants to   take the   eight o'clock   plane.
Joe wants to   take the   bus.
Bob wants to   take the   six o'clock   train.
Bill wants to   come with   us.

R WHAT TIME IS IT?

Draw the time on the clocks.

1. It's ten o'clock.   2. It's five fifteen.   3. It's nine thirty.   4. It's three forty-five.

5. It's noon.   6. It's half past eleven.   7. It's a quarter to one.   8. It's a quarter after two.

S WHICH TIMES ARE CORRECT?

Circle the correct times.

1. a. It's four o'clock.
   b. It's five o'clock.

2. a. It's eleven thirteen.
   b. It's eleven thirty.

3. a. It's a quarter after nine.
   b. It's three fifteen.

4. a. It's noon.
   b. It's midnight.

5. a. It's half past six.
   b. It's twelve thirty.

6. a. It's two fifteen.
   b. It's a quarter to three.

7. a. It's one thirty.
   b. It's one forty-five.

8. a. It's a quarter to seven.
   b. It's a quarter after seven.

9. a. It's six o'clock.
   b. It's midnight.

T LISTENING

Listen and write the time you hear.

1. ___7:45___   4. _____   7. _____   10. _____

2. _____   5. _____   8. _____   11. _____

3. _____   6. _____   9. _____   12. _____

U ALAN CHANG'S DAY

Alan Chang gets up every day at seven fifteen. He brushes his teeth and takes a shower. At seven forty-five he eats breakfast and reads his e-mail. At eight thirty he leaves the house and drives to work. Alan works at a computer company. He begins work at nine o'clock. Every day he uses business software on the computer and talks to people on the telephone. At twelve o'clock Alan is always hungry and thirsty. He eats lunch in the cafeteria. Alan leaves work at five thirty. He eats dinner at six o'clock and then at half past seven he watches videos on his new DVD player.

1. What time does Alan get up every day?   _He gets up at 7:15._

2. What time does he eat breakfast?   _____

3. What time does he leave the house?   _____

4. What time does he begin work?   _____

5. Where does Alan work?   _____

6. What does he do at noon?   _____

7. What does he do at half past five?   _____

8. What time does he eat dinner?   _____

9. What does he do at seven thirty?   _____

V YOUR DAY

Answer in complete sentences.

1. What time do you usually get up?   ....

2. What do you do after you get up?   ....

3. When do you usually leave for school or work?   ....

4. What time do you usually have lunch?   ....

5. When do you get home from school or work?   ....

6. What time do you usually have dinner?   ....

7. What do you usually do after dinner?   ....

8. When do you usually go to bed?   ....

Listen. Then clap and practice.

Time flies.
The days go by.
Monday, Tuesday,
Wednesday, Thursday,
Friday, Saturday.
Time flies.
The days go by.

Time flies.
The months go by.
January, February, March, April,
May, June, July, August,
September, October, November, December.
Time flies.
The months go by.

The seasons come,
The seasons go.
Autumn, winter, spring, summer,
Autumn, winter, spring, summer.
Time flies.
The years go by.
Where do they go?
I don't know.

Listen and fill in the words to the song. Then listen again and sing along.

I'm	going	be	after	day	year	December	April	right
it's	wait	in	past	month	fall	February	July	
you	waiting	to	with	week	summer	September		

Any day, any ___week___ 1 , any month, any _____ 2 , I'm _____ _____ 3

wait right here to be with you.

_____ 4 the spring, in the _____ 5 , in the winter, or the _____ 6 , just call.

I'm _____ 7 here to be with you.

_____ _____ 8 to wait from January, _____ 9 March,

_____ 10 , May, June and _____ 11 , August, _____ 12 , October,

and November, and all of _____ 13 . I'm going to wait . . .

_____ 14 one o'clock, a quarter _____ 15 . It's half _____ 16 one, a quarter

_____ 17 two. And I'm going _____ _____ 18 right here to be with you.

Any _____ 19 , any week, any _____ 20 , any year, I'm going to wait

_____ 21 here to be _____ 22 you.

Yes, I'm going to wait right here _____ _____ 23 with _____ 24 .

✓ **CHECK-UP TEST: Chapters 13–14**

A.

Ex. Ted _____wants to go skating_____, but ____he can't____. He ____has to fix his car____.

1. We _____, but _____. We _____.

2. Alice _____, but _____. She _____.

3. I _____, but _____. I _____.

B. Fill in the blanks.

| is | are | do | does |

Ex. When __is__ Harry going to leave the house?

1. When _____ you going to call the mechanic?

2. _____ you have a bad cold?

3. What _____ they going to do this evening?

4. Where _____ you going skiing?

5. What _____ Carol have to do this Tuesday?

6. _____ your son going to take a bath today?

C. *Ex.* Tom wants to move next spring. _____He doesn't want to move_____ this fall.

Dad is going to fix the sink. _____He isn't going to fix_____ the car.

1. I want to teach French. _____ English.

2. We're going to bed at 10:00. _____ at 9:00.

3. Mrs. Miller can bake pies. _____ cakes.

4. Frank has to go to the dentist. _____ the doctor.

5. Jim and Julie can speak Japanese. _____ Spanish.

6. We have to do our homework. _____ our exercises.

112   Activity Workbook

D. Every day Helen gets up at 7:30. At 8:00 she eats breakfast, and at 8:30 she goes to work. At noon she has lunch, and at 5:00 she takes the bus home. What's Helen going to do tomorrow?

Tomorrow Helen _____ *is going to get up* _____ at 7:30. At 8:00 she's

_____¹ breakfast, and at 8:30 _____² to work. At noon

_____³ lunch, and at 5:00 _____⁴ home.

E. Write the question.

What	When	Where

Ex. I'm going to clean my house <u>this evening</u>. _____*When are you going to clean your house?*_____

1. She's going to <u>fix her sink</u> tomorrow. _____

2. He's going to play tennis <u>in the park</u>. _____

3. I'm going to go to the zoo <u>this weekend</u>. _____

4. They're going to study <u>Spanish</u> next year. _____

F. What time is it?

Ex.

It's ten o'clock.

1.

It's five fifteen.

2.

It's nine thirty.

3.

It's noon.

4.

It's two forty-five.

5.

It's a quarter after eleven.

G. Listen to the story. Fill in the correct times.

English	_____	Chinese	_____	lunch	_____
mathematics	_____	science	_____	music	_____

15

A WHAT'S THE MATTER?

backache	cough	fever	sore throat	toothache
cold	earache	headache	stomachache	

1. He _____has a cold_____

_____.

2. She _____

_____.

3. I _____

_____.

4. She _____

_____.

5. I _____

_____.

6. He _____

_____.

7. She _____

_____.

8. You _____

_____.

9. He _____

_____.

B LISTENING

Listen to the story. Put the number under the correct picture.

_____

___1___

_____

_____

_____

_____

_____

_____

C GRAMMARRAP: *What's the Matter?*

Listen. Then clap and practice.

A.   What's the matter with   you?

B.   I have a headache.

What's the matter with   YOU?

A.   I have a cold.

A.   What's the matter with   him?

B.   He has a toothache.

What's the matter with   HER?

A.   She has a cold.

A.   What's the matter with   Mary?

B.   She has an earache.

What's the matter with   BILL?

A.   He has a very bad   cold.

A.   What's the matter with   Fred?

B.   He has a backache.

What's the matter with   ANNE?

A.   She has an awful   cold.

A.   What's the matter with   Jane?

B.   She has a stomachache.

What's the matter with   PAUL?

A.   He has a terrible   cold.

A.   What's the matter with the   students?

B.   They have sore   throats.

What's the matter with the   teachers?

A.   They have terrible   colds.

They have terrible   terrible

colds!

bake	cook	dance	rest	shout	study
clean	cry	paint	shave	smile	type

1. I _____cooked_____ .

2. I _____ .

3. I _____ .

4. I _____ .

5. I _____ .

6. I _____ .

7. I _____ .

8. I _____ .

9. I _____ .

10. I _____ .

11. I _____ .

12. I _____ .

brush	cook	paint	plant	play	study	wait	watch	work

1. I _____work_____ in an office every day.

2. I _____played_____ the guitar yesterday.

3. I _____ my teeth every day.

4. I _____ flowers yesterday.

5. I _____ dinner every day.

6. I _____ English yesterday.

7. I _____ my fence yesterday.

8. I _____ TV every day.

9. I _____ for the bus yesterday.

F **LISTENING**

Listen and circle the correct answer.

Ex. I study. yesterday / (every day)   I played cards. (yesterday) / every day

1. yesterday / every day
2. yesterday / every day
3. yesterday / every day
4. yesterday / every day
5. yesterday / every day
6. yesterday / every day
7. yesterday / every day
8. yesterday / every day
9. yesterday / every day
10. yesterday / every day
11. yesterday / every day
12. yesterday / every day

bark	clean	cry	drink	eat	ride	sing	sit	skate	write

1. A. What did James do today?

   B. _____He cleaned_____ his apartment all day.

2. A. What did your sister do today?

   B. _____ letters all morning.

3. A. What did Mr. and Mrs. Porter do yesterday?

   B. _____ songs all evening.

4. A. What did you and your friends do today?

   B. _____ in the park all afternoon.

5. A. What did Linda do yesterday?

   B. _____ lemonade all morning.

6. A. What did Jimmy do today?

   B. _____ candy and cookies all day.

7. A. What did Mrs. Mason's children do today?

   B. _____ all afternoon.

8. A. What did the neighbors' dogs do yesterday?

   B. _____ all night.

9. A. What did Howard do yesterday?

   B. _____ in the clinic all evening.

10. A. What did Grandma do today?

    B. _____ her bicycle all afternoon.

H PUZZLE

Across

3. ride
4. study
6. eat

Down

1. cry
2. work
4. sit
5. drink

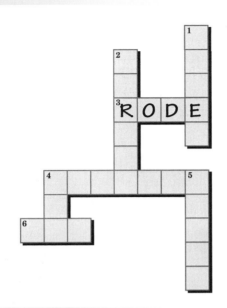

I PETER'S DAY AT HOME

| bake | cook | fix | paint | plant | rest | wash |

1. Thank you, Peter. This is a very good dinner.

3. Look at the car! It's really clean. Thank you.

5. The kitchen looks beautiful. Yellow is my favorite color.

2. This is a wonderful cake, Peter.

4. The new flowers in the garden are beautiful.

6. The sink isn't broken! I can brush my teeth in the bathroom now!

What did Peter do today?

1. _____He cooked dinner._____   2. _____

3. _____   4. _____

5. _____   6. _____

What did Peter do after dinner?

7. _____

washed [t]	cleaned [d]	painted [ɪd]

A. What did you   do   today?

B. I washed my   floors.

A. Your floors?   **B.** Yes!

B. I washed my   floors all   day!

A. What did Mark   do   today?

B. He cleaned his   house.

A. His house?   **B.** Yes!

B. He cleaned his   house all   day!

A. What did Pam   do   today?

B. She painted her   porch.

A. Her porch?   **B.** Yes!

B. She painted her   porch all   day!

A. What did they   do   today?

B. They sang some   songs.

A. Some songs?   **B.** Yes!

They sang some   songs all   day!

A. What did you   do   today?

B. I _____.

A. _____? **B.** Yes!

B. I _____ all day!

K MY GRANDFATHER'S BIRTHDAY PARTY

At my grandfather's birthday party last night, everybody (listen) _____listened_____ ¹ to

Mexican music and (dance) _____². My sister Gloria (sing) _____³ my

grandfather's favorite songs all evening, and my brother Daniel (play) _____⁴ the

guitar.

Everybody (sit) _____⁵ in the living room with my grandmother and grandfather

and (look) _____⁶ at old photographs. We (laugh) _____⁷, we (smile)

_____⁸, we (cry) _____⁹, and we (talk) _____¹⁰about "the good

old days." What did I do at my grandfather's birthday party? I (drink) _____¹¹

lemonade and (eat) _____¹² a lot of food!

L MATCHING

__e__ 1. At the party my brother played _____.

_____ 2. Everybody sat and talked about _____.

_____ 3. My sister has a sore throat today because _____.

_____ 4. We all looked at _____.

_____ 5. We listened to _____.

_____ 6. I have a toothache today because I _____.

_____ 7. I also have a stomachache because I _____.

a. drank lemonade all night

b. Mexican music

c. "the good old days"

d. ate a lot of food

e. the guitar

f. old photographs

g. she sang all evening

A CORRECT THE SENTENCE

1. Jennifer brushed her teeth last night.

   She didn't brush her teeth.

   She brushed her hair.

2. Kevin played the violin yesterday afternoon.

   _____

   _____

3. Harold and Betty listened to the news yesterday evening.

   _____

   _____

4. Mrs. Martinez waited for the train this afternoon.

   _____

   _____

5. Frank fixed his fence yesterday morning.

   _____

   _____

6. Mr. and Mrs. Park cleaned their attic today.

   _____

   _____

7. Marvin baked a pie yesterday evening.

   _____

   _____

8. Patty called her grandmother last night.

   _____

   _____

ALAN AND HIS SISTER

Alan and his sister Ellen did very different things yesterday. Alan (rest) ____rested____ [1] all

day. He didn't (work) _____ [2], and he didn't (study) _____ [3]. He (listen)

_____ [4] to music yesterday morning. He (watch) _____ [5] game shows on TV

yesterday afternoon. And yesterday evening he (talk) _____ [6] to his friends on the

telephone and (play) _____ [7] games on his computer.

Ellen didn't (listen) _____ [8] to music. She didn't (watch) _____ [9] game shows on

TV, and she didn't (play) _____ [10] games on her computer What did she do? She (study)

_____ [11] English yesterday morning. She (clean) _____ [12] the yard yesterday

afternoon. And she (cook) _____ [13] dinner for her family last night.

C **YES AND NO**

1. Did Alan rest all day yesterday?   _____Yes, he did._____

2. Did Ellen rest all day yesterday?   _____No, she didn't._____

3. Did Ellen study yesterday morning?   _____

4. Did Alan study yesterday morning?   _____

5. Did Alan watch TV yesterday afternoon?   _____

6. ____Did Ellen clean____ the yard yesterday afternoon?   Yes, she did.

7. _____ to his friends yesterday evening?   Yes, he did.

8. _____ dinner for his family last night?   No, he didn't.

9. _____ to music yesterday morning?   No, she didn't.

10. _____ game shows yesterday afternoon?   No, she didn't.

11. _____ English yesterday afternoon?   No, he didn't.

WHAT DID THEY DO?

1. I didn't buy a car. I ____bought____ a motorcycle.

2. Michael didn't have a headache. He _____ a toothache.

3. Alice didn't write to her uncle. She _____ to her cousin.

4. We didn't do our homework last night. We _____ yoga.

5. They didn't take the bus to work today. They _____ the train.

6. Barbara didn't get up at 7:00 this morning. She _____ up at 6:00.

7. My friend and I didn't go swimming yesterday. We _____ bowling.

8. Martha didn't read the newspaper last night. She _____ a book.

9. My children didn't make breakfast this morning. They _____ lunch.

E **THEY DIDN'T DO WHAT THEY USUALLY DO**

1. Robert usually writes to his friends.
   He ____didn't____ ____write____ to his friends yesterday.
   He ____wrote____ to his grandparents.

2. I usually have a cold in January.
   I _____ _____ a cold last January.
   I _____ a cold last July.

3. We usually eat at home on Friday night.
   We _____ _____ at home last Friday night.
   We _____ at a very nice restaurant.

4. Bill usually gets up 7:00 o'clock.
   He _____ _____ up at 7:00 this morning.
   He _____ up at 10:00.

5. Tom and Tina usually go dancing every week.
   They _____ _____ dancing this week.
   They _____ sailing.

6. Susie usually drinks milk every afternoon.
   She _____ _____ milk this afternoon.
   She _____ lemonade.

7. My brother usually makes lunch on Sunday.
   He _____ _____ lunch last Sunday.
   He _____ dinner.

8. Mr. Lee usually takes his wife to the movies.
   He _____ _____ his wife to the movies last night.
   He _____ his daughter and his son-in-law.

9. We usually buy food at a large supermarket.
   We _____ _____ food at a supermarket today.
   We _____ food at a small grocery store.

10. I usually sit next to Maria in English class.
    I _____ _____ next to Maria yesterday.
    I _____ next to her sister Carmen.

A.   Did she wash her   skirt?

B.   No, she   didn't.

A.   What did she   wash?

B.   She washed her __shirt__ .

A.   Did they paint the   door?

B.   No, they   didn't.

A.   What did they paint?

B.   They painted the _____ .

A.   Did he call his   mother?

B.   No, he   didn't.

A.   Who did he   call?

B.   He called his _____ .

A.   Did you buy   new suits?

B.   No, we   didn't.

A.   What did you   buy?

B.   We bought new _____ .

A.   Did you get up at   seven?

B.   No, I   didn't.

A.   When did you get   up?

B.   I got up at _____ .

G WHAT'S THE ANSWER?

1. Did Henry ride his bicycle to work this morning?   Yes, _____*he did*_____.

2. Did you get up at 6:00 this morning?   No, _____.

3. Did your sister call you last night?   Yes, _____.

4. Did Mr. and Mrs. Chen clean their apartment last weekend?   No, _____.

5. Did you and your friends go to the library yesterday afternoon?   Yes, _____.

6. Did your father make spaghetti for dinner last night?   No, _____.

7. Excuse me. Did I take your gloves?   Yes, _____.

8. Bob, did you do your exercises today?   No, _____.

H WHAT'S THE QUESTION?

1. _____*Did she buy*_____ a car?   No, she didn't. She bought a truck.

2. _____ a headache?   No, he didn't. He had a backache.

3. _____ a shower?   No, I didn't. I took a bath.

4. _____ to the supermarket?   No, they didn't. They went to the bank.

5. _____ in the living room?   No, we didn't. We sat in the kitchen.

6. _____ a right turn?   No, you didn't. You made a left turn.

I LISTENING

Listen and choose the correct response.

1. a. I write to her every day.
   b. I wrote to her this morning. *(circled)*

2. a. He washes it every weekend.
   b. He washed it last weekend.

3. a. They visit my aunt and my uncle.
   b. They visited my aunt and my uncle.

4. a. She did yoga in the park.
   b. She does yoga in the park.

5. a. He went to sleep at 8:00.
   b. He goes to sleep at 8:00.

6. a. We clean it every weekend.
   b. We cleaned it last weekend.

7. a. We take them to the zoo.
   b. We took them to the zoo.

8. a. I make spaghetti.
   b. I made spaghetti.

9. a. She reads it every afternoon.
   b. She read it this afternoon.

10. a. I get up at 7:00.
    b. I got up at 7:00.

J I'M SORRY I'M LATE!

forget	go	have to	miss
get up	have	meet	steal

1. I _____missed_____ the train.

2. I _____ a headache.

3. I _____ my lunch.

4. I _____ my girlfriend on the way to work.

5. I _____ late.

6. A thief _____ my bicycle.

7. I _____ go to the bank.

8. I _____ to sleep on the bus.

K MATCHING

_d_	1. buy	a.	wrote	___	7. get	g.	had
___	2. steal	b.	did	___	8. eat	h.	drove
___	3. do	c.	went	___	9. have	i.	made
___	4. see	d.	bought	___	10. forget	j.	got
___	5. go	e.	saw	___	11. make	k.	forgot
___	6. write	f.	stole	___	12. drive	l.	ate

L **GRAMMARRAP:** *Old Friends*

Listen. Then clap and practice.

We walked and   talked

And talked and   walked.

Walked and   talked,

Talked and   walked.

We sat in the   garden

And looked at the   flowers.

We talked and   talked

For hours and   hours.

He drank   milk,

And I drank   tea.

We talked and   talked

From one to   three.

We talked about him.

We talked about us.

Then we walked to the corner

To get the   bus.

We waited and   waited.

The bus was   late.

So we stood and   talked

From four to   eight.

M **GRAMMARRAP:** *Gossip*

Listen. Then clap and practice.

I told   Jack.

Jack told   Jill.

Jill told   Fred.

Fred told   Bill.

Bill called   Anne.

Anne called   Sue.

Sue told   Jim.

But who told   you?

was	were

We _____were_____ [1] very upset at work last Friday. Our computers _____ [2] broken, our boss _____ [3] angry because he _____ [4] tired, and my friends and I _____ [5] sick. Outside it _____ [6] cloudy and it _____ [7] very cold. And then in the afternoon all the trains _____ [8] late. I _____ [9] hungry when I got home, and my children _____ [10] very noisy. It _____ [11] a terrible day!

We _____were_____ [12] very happy at work on Monday. Our computers _____ [13] fine, our boss _____ [14] happy, and my friends and I _____ [15] energetic. Outside it _____ [16] sunny, it _____ [17] warm, and all the trains _____ [18] early. My children _____ [19] very quiet when I got home. We ate a big dinner, and I _____ [20] very full. It was a wonderful day!

B **LISTENING**

Listen and circle the word you hear.

1.	(is) / was	4.	is / was	7.	are / were	10.	is / was
2.	is / was	5.	is / was	8.	are / were	11.	are / were
3.	are / were	6.	are / were	9.	is / was	12.	are / were

| clean | enormous | happy | shiny | thin |
| comfortable | full | healthy | tall | |

1. Before I took A-1 Vitamins, I __was__ always

   sick. Now __I'm__ __healthy__ .

2. Before Harold met Gertrude, he _____ sad.

   Now _____ _____ all the time.

3. Before we ate a big breakfast today, we _____

   hungry. Now _____ _____ .

4. Before Helen got her new sofa, she _____

   uncomfortable. Now _____ very _____ .

5. Before you drank A-1 Skim Milk, you _____

   heavy. Now _____ _____ .

6. Before Charlie used A-1 Car Wax, his car _____

   dull. Now _____ _____ .

7. Before these children used A-1 soap, they

   _____ dirty. Now _____ _____ .

8. When I _____ young, I _____ very short.

   Now _____ _____ .

9. Before we bought A-1 Bird Food, our birds _____

   very tiny. Now _____ _____ .

D WHAT'S THE WORD?

1. A. ___Were___ you at a concert last night?

   B. No, I ___wasn't___. I ___was___ at a play.

2. A. _____ your neighbors quiet last Saturday night?

   B. No, they _____. They _____ very noisy.

3. A. _____ your boss in the office yesterday?

   B. No, she _____. She _____ on vacation.

4. A. _____ we at home last Tuesday?

   B. No, we _____. We _____ at the mall.

5. A. _____ the questions on the examination easy?

   B. No, they _____. They _____ very difficult.

6. A. _____ Timothy on time for his wedding?

   B. No, he _____. He _____ late.

E LISTENING

Listen and circle the word you hear.

1. was
   (wasn't)

2. were
   weren't

3. were
   weren't

4. was
   wasn't

5. was
   wasn't

6. were
   weren't

7. were
   weren't

8. was
   wasn't

did	was	were
didn't	wasn't	weren't

A. Why _____did_____ ¹ Victor leave the party early?

B. He _____ ² like the party. It _____ ³ noisy, the food _____ ⁴ very good, and his friends _____ ⁵ there.

A. Where _____ ⁶ you last week? You _____ ⁷ at work.

B. That's right. I _____ ⁸.

A. _____ ⁹ you sick?

B. Yes, I _____ ¹⁰. I _____ ¹¹ very sick. I had an earache and a cold.

A. _____ ¹² you also have a headache?

B. No. I _____ ¹³ have a headache, but I had a sore throat. I _____ ¹⁴ go to work all week. I _____ ¹⁵ really sick!

A. How _____ ¹⁶ your vacation?

B. It _____ ¹⁷ terrible!

A. That's too bad. _____ ¹⁸ you like the hotel?

B. No, we _____ ¹⁹. The bathroom sink _____ ²⁰ broken, the hotel room _____ ²¹ clean, and we _____ ²² sleep well at night because the people in the next room _____ ²³ very loud.

A. _____ ²⁴ you swim at the beach?

B. No, we _____ ²⁵. The weather _____ ²⁶ very cold!

A. _____ ²⁷ your grandchildren visit you last weekend?

B. No, they _____ ²⁸.

A. That's too bad. _____ ²⁹ they busy?

B. My grandson _____ ³⁰ feel well, and my granddaughter _____ ³¹ on a business trip. We _____ ³² sad because we _____ ³³ see them.

Listen. Then clap and practice.

A.   Were you late this   morning?

B.   No, I wasn't. I was   early.

A.   Was he sick last   night?

B.   No, he wasn't. He was   fine.

A.   Was her hair very   straight?

B.   No, it wasn't. It was   curly.

A.   Were there eight new   lessons?

B.   No, there weren't. There were   nine.

A.   Was the movie   short?

B.   No, it wasn't. It was   long.

A.   Was the food   expensive?

B.   No, it wasn't. It was   free.

A.   Was I right?

B.   No, you weren't. You were   wrong.

A.   Were the tickets two   dollars?

B.   No, they weren't.   They were three.

WHAT ARE THEY SAYING?

basketball	did	freckles	short	subjects	wasn't	weren't
curly	didn't	hobby	sports	was	were	

A. Tell me, what ___did___ ¹ you look like when you _____ ² young? _____ ³ you tall?

B. No, I _____ ⁴. I _____ ⁵ _____ ⁶.

A. _____ ⁷ you have straight hair?

B. No, I _____ ⁸. I had _____ ⁹ hair.

A. Oh. And _____ ¹⁰ you have dimples?

B. No, I _____ ¹¹, but I had _____ ¹².

A. I'm sure you _____ ¹³ very cute!

   What _____ ¹⁴ you do with your friends?

B. We played sports.

A. Oh. What _____ ¹⁵ you play?

B. We played _____ ¹⁶ and tennis.

A. Tell me, _____ ¹⁷ you like school?

B. Yes. I liked school a lot.

A. What _____ ¹⁸ your favorite _____ ¹⁹?

B. English and mathematics.

A. _____ ²⁰ you have a _____ ²¹?

B. Yes, I _____ ²². I played chess.

LISTENING

Listen and choose the correct response.

1. a. I was born last week.
   b. I was born in Japan. *(circled)*

2. a. Yes, I did.
   b. I grew up in Tokyo.

3. a. English.
   b. No, I didn't.

4. a. In Los Angeles.
   b. Last year.

5. a. I was tall and thin.
   b. I didn't look.

6. a. No. I had straight hair.
   b. No. I had dimples.

7. a. I played sports.
   b. I play chess.

8. a. Yes. I'm here.
   b. Yes. My father.

Listen. Then clap and practice.

A. The teacher was   there,

But where were the   students?

B. The students were   there.

All.   Where?

A. The teacher was   there,

The students were   there,

But where were the   books?

B. The books were   there.

All.   Where?

A. The teacher was   there,

The students were   there,

The books were   there,

But where was the   chalk?

B. The chalk was   there.

All.   Where?

A. The teacher was   there,

The students were   there,

The books were   there,

The chalk was   there,

But where were the   chairs?

B. The chairs were   there.

All.   Where?

B.   There.

All.   Where?

B. Right there!

Right   there!

✓ **CHECK-UP TEST: Chapters 15–17**

A. Fill in the blanks.

was	were	wasn't	weren't

1. A. ___Was___ Barbara at work yesterday?

   B. No, she _____ . She _____ sick.

2. A. Why _____ you late today?

   B. I _____ late because I _____ on time for the bus.

3. A. Where _____ Grandma and Grandpa last night? They _____ at home.

   B. They _____ at a concert.

B. Complete the sentences.

Ex. Before we washed our car, it ___was___ dirty. Now ___it's___ ___clean___ .

1. Before I ate dinner, I _____ hungry. Now _____ _____ .

2. When I got my cats, they _____ tiny. Now _____ _____ .

3. When we _____ in college, we _____ thin. Now _____ _____ .

4. When I was young, I _____ energetic. Now _____ _____ .

C. Complete the sentences.

Ex. a. Carla usually studies English.
   She ___didn't___ ___study___ English yesterday.
   She ___studied___ mathematics.

   b. Paul usually writes to his friends.
   He ___didn't___ ___write___ to his friends yesterday.
   He ___wrote___ to his cousins.

1. I usually drive to the park on Saturday.
   I _____ _____ to the park last Saturday.
   I _____ to the mall.

2. We usually arrive late.
   We _____ _____ late today.
   We _____ on time.

3. My husband and my son usually shave in the morning.
   They _____ _____ in the morning today.
   They _____ in the afternoon.

4. Bob usually goes jogging in the evening.
   He _____ _____ jogging yesterday evening.
   He _____ dancing.

5. Margaret usually reads the newspaper in the morning.
   She _____ _____ the newspaper yesterday morning.
   She _____ a magazine.

D. Write the question.

Ex. _____Did they get up_____ at 8:00?   No, they didn't. They got up at 10:00.

1. _____ his brother?   No, he didn't. He met his sister.

2. _____ her bicycle?   No, she didn't. She rode her motorcycle.

3. _____ a good time?   No, we didn't. We had a terrible time.

4. _____ lunch?   No, they didn't. They made dinner.

5. _____ a movie?   No, I didn't. I saw a play.

E. Read the story and then write about yesterday.

Every morning I get up early. I brush my teeth, and I do my exercises. Then I sit in the kitchen and I eat breakfast. At 8:00 I go to work. I walk to the drug store and I buy a newspaper. Then I take the train to my office. I don't take the bus, and I don't drive my car.

Yesterday I _____got up_____ early. I _____[1] my teeth, and I _____[2] my exercises. Then I _____[3] in the kitchen and I _____[4] breakfast. At 8:00 I _____[5] to work. I _____[6] to the drug store and I _____[7] a newspaper. Then I _____[8] the train to my office. I _____ _____[9] the bus, and I _____ _____[10] my car.

F. Listen and circle the word you hear.

Ex.	(is) / was	3.	is / was	6.	are / were
1.	is / was	4.	are / were	7.	is / was
2.	are / were	5.	is / was	8.	are / were

Listening Scripts

Page 3 Exercise C

Listen and circle the number you hear.

1. My address is five Main Street.
2. My address is seven Main Street.
3. My address is two Main Street.
4. My address is six Main Street.
5. My address is one Main Street.
6. My address is three Main Street.
7. My address is four Main Street.
8. My address is eight Main Street.
9. My address is ten Main Street.
10. My address is nine Main Street.

Page 4 Exercise E

Listen and write the missing numbers.

1. A. What's your phone number?
   B. My phone number is 389-7932.
2. A. What's your telephone number?
   B. My telephone number is 837-2953.
3. A. What's your apartment number?
   B. My apartment number is 6-B.
4. A. What's your address?
   B. My address is 10 Main Street.
5. A. What's your fax number?
   B. My fax number is 654-7315.
6. A. What's your license number?
   B. My license number is 2613498.

Page 5 Exercise F

Listen and write the missing letters.

1. A. What's your last name?
   B. Carter.
   A. How do you spell that?
   B. C-A-R-T-E-R.
2. A. What's your last name?
   B. Johnson.
   A. How do you spell that?
   B. J-O-H-N-S-O-N.
3. A. What's your first name?
   B. Gerald.
   A. How do you spell that?
   B. G-E-R-A-L-D.
4. A. What's your last name?
   B. Anderson.
   A. How do you spell that?
   B. A-N-D-E-R-S-O-N.
5. A. What's your first name?
   B. Phillip.
   A. How do you spell that?
   B. P-H-I-L-L-I-P.
6. A. What's your last name?
   B. Martinez.
   A. How do you spell that?
   B. M-A-R-T-I-N-E-Z.

Page 6 Exercise B

Listen and put a check under the correct picture.

1. A. Where's the book?
   B. It's on the desk.
2. A. Where's the dictionary?
   B. It's on the chair.
3. A. Where's the ruler?
   B. It's on the desk.
4. A. Where's the map?
   B. It's on the bulletin board.
5. A. Where's the globe?
   B. It's on the bookshelf.

6. A. Where's the computer?
   B. It's on the table.

Page 11 Exercise J

Listen and write the number under the correct picture.

1. Our English teacher is in the hospital.
2. Mr. and Mrs. Sanchez are in the restaurant.
3. Mary is at the dentist.
4. Billy and Jimmy are in the park.
5. Mr. and Mrs. Lee are at the social security office.
6. James is home in bed.

Page 11 Exercise K

Listen and circle the word you hear.

1. Where are you?
2. Ms. Jones is in the bank.
3. We're friends.
4. Hi. How are you?
5. Where's the newspaper?
6. He's from Korea.
7. The computer is on the table.
8. It's in the bathroom.

Page 15 Exercise C

Listen and put a check under the correct picture.

1. He's eating lunch.
2. We're drinking milk.
3. I'm playing the guitar.
4. She's playing the piano.
5. We're cooking breakfast.
6. It's in the classroom.
7. I'm reading.
8. He's watching TV.
9. She's studying mathematics.
10. They're playing baseball in the yard.

Page 20 Exercise D

Listen and write the letter or number you hear.

Ex. A. What's your first name?
    B. Mark.
    A. How do you spell that?
    B. M-A-R-K.

1. A. What's your last name?
   B. Carter.
   A. How do you spell that?
   B. C-A-R-T-E-R.
2. A. What's your telephone number?
   B. My telephone number is 354-9812.
3. A. What's your fax number?
   B. My fax number is 890-7462.
4. A. What's your first name?
   B. Julie.
   A. How do you spell that?
   B. J-U-L-I-E.
5. A. What's your telephone number?
   B. My telephone number is 672-3059.
6. A. What's your license number?
   B. My license number is 5170349.

Page 22 Exercise C

Listen and circle the word you hear.

1. We're cleaning our room.
2. He's doing his homework.
3. She's washing her hair.
4. They're fixing their car.
5. You're fixing your TV.
6. I'm feeding my cat.

Page 24 Exercise G

Listen and circle the word you hear.

1. He's studying.
2. She's doing her homework.
3. I'm feeding my cat.

4. He's cleaning his yard.
5. We're fixing our car.
6. They're washing their clothes.

Page 27 Exercise C

Listen and circle the word you hear.

1. Sally's brother is very tall.
2. Their dog is very heavy.
3. The questions in my English book are very easy.
4. My friend George is single.
5. Mary's cat is very ugly!
6. This book is very cheap.

Page 32 Exercise K

Listen and circle the word you hear.

1. A. How's the weather in Rome today?
   B. It's cool.
2. A. How's the weather in Tokyo today?
   B. It's snowing.
3. A. How's the weather in Seoul today?
   B. It's sunny.
4. A. How's the weather in Shanghai today?
   B. It's hot.
5. A. How's the weather in New York today?
   B. It's raining.
6. A. How's the weather in Miami today?
   B. It's cloudy.

Page 34 Exercise O

Listen to the temperature in Fahrenheit and Celsius. Write the numbers you hear.

1. In Los Angeles, it's 86° Fahrenheit/30° Celsius.
2. In Seoul, it's 32° Fahrenheit/0° Celsius.
3. In San Juan, it's 81° Fahrenheit/27° Celsius.
4. In Hong Kong, it's 72° Fahrenheit/22° Celsius.
5. In Miami, it's 93° Fahrenheit/34° Celsius.
6. In London, it's 56° Fahrenheit/13° Celsius.
7. In Mexico City, it's 66° Fahrenheit/19° Celsius.
8. In Moscow, it's 34° Fahrenheit/1° Celsius.

Page 36 Exercise B

Listen and put a check under the correct picture.

1. In this photograph, my sister is skateboarding in the park.
2. In this photograph, my son is acting in a play.
3. In this photograph, my friends are dancing at my wedding.
4. In this photograph, my uncle is baking a cake.
5. In this photograph, my cousin is playing a game on her computer.
6. In this photograph, my husband is standing in front of our apartment building.
7. In this photograph, my grandparents are having dinner.
8. In this photograph, my aunt is planting flowers.

Page 40 Exercise E

Listen and choose the correct response.

Ex. Is he old?

1. Is it large?
2. Is she poor?
3. Is it sunny?
4. Is he quiet?

Page 43 Exercise C

Listen to the sentences about the buildings on the map. After each sentence, write the name on the correct building.

1. There's a bakery between the barber shop and the bank.
2. There's a school next to the church.
3. There's a department store across from the school and the church.
4. There's a library around the corner from the barber shop.
5. There's a hospital across from the library.
6. There's a police station next to the hospital.
7. There's a hair salon across from the barber shop.
8. There's a supermarket next to the hair salon.
9. There's a video store around the corner from the bank.

10. There's a park between the library and the video store.
11. There's a health club around the corner from the department store.
12. There's a train station across from the health club.

Page 51 Exercise D

Listen and circle the word you hear.

1. umbrellas
2. blouses
3. coats
4. computer
5. shoes
6. exercises
7. dress
8. restaurants
9. necklaces
10. earring
11. belt
12. watches
13. nieces
14. nephew
15. shirts
16. tie

Page 52 Exercise E

Listen and circle the color you hear.

1. My favorite color is blue.
2. My favorite color is green.
3. My favorite color is gray.
4. My favorite color is silver.
5. My favorite color is yellow.
6. My favorite color is orange.

Page 54 Exercise H

Listen and put a check under the correct picture.

1. I'm washing these socks.
2. He's reading this book.
3. I'm looking for these men.
4. They're using these computers.
5. We're vacuuming this rug.
6. She's playing with these dogs.
7. We're painting this garage.
8. They're listening to these radios.

Page 54 Exercise I

Listen and circle the correct word to complete the sentence.

1. This bicycle . . .
2. These exercises . . .
3. These apartment buildings . . .
4. This bracelet . . .
5. These women . . .
6. These sunglasses . . .
7. This car . . .
8. These jeans . . .
9. This refrigerator . . .

Page 61 Exercise F

Listen and circle the correct word to complete the sentence.

Ex. These dresses . . .

1. That house . . .
2. Those people . . .
3. These flowers . . .
4. This blouse . . .

Page 63 Exercise B

Listen and choose the correct response.

1. What's your name?
2. What language do you speak?
3. What do they do every day?
4. Where do you live?
5. What language do you speak?
6. What do you do every day?

Page 66 Exercise G

Listen and circle the word you hear.

1. We live in Paris.
2. Where do you live?
3. What language does he speak?
4. Every day I listen to Greek music.
5. Every day she watches English TV shows.
6. What do they eat every day?
7. Every day I sing Korean songs.
8. Every day she eats Chinese food.
9. Every day he reads Mexican newspapers.

Activity Workbook **139**

Page 70 Exercise D

Listen and choose the correct response.

1. What kind of food do you like?
2. Do they paint houses?
3. Why does he go to that restaurant?
4. When does Mrs. Miller cook dinner?
5. Do you work in a bank?
6. Where do they live?
7. What do your children do in the park?
8. Does your friend Patty drive a taxi?
9. Why do they shop in that store?

Page 72 Exercise I

Listen and choose the correct response.

1. Do you do a different kind of sport every day?
2. Does Bob write for the school newspaper?
3. Do Mr. and Mrs. Chang live near a bus stop?
4. Does your sister baby-sit every weekend?
5. Does Timmy do a different activity every day?
6. Do your children play in the orchestra?
7. Does your son sing in the choir?
8. Do your parents go to the park every day?
9. Do you play cards with your friends?

Page 75 Exercise D

Listen and choose the correct response.

Ex. What do Patty and Peter do during the week?

1. When do you watch your favorite TV program?
2. Why do you eat Italian food?
3. Does Carlos visit his grandparents in Puerto Rico?
4. What kind of books do you like?
5. Where do your nephews live?

Page 77 Exercise C

Listen and put a check under the correct picture.

1. How often do you read them?
2. I call her every day.
3. I don't like him.
4. I wash it every weekend.
5. He calls us all the time.
6. I say "hello" to them every morning.

Page 78 Exercise G

Listen and choose the correct answer.

1. Henry's car is always very dirty.
2. My husband sometimes makes dinner.
3. My neighbors play loud music at night.
4. My grandparents rarely speak English.
5. Jane always spends a lot of time with her friends.
6. I rarely study in the library.

Page 82 Exercise N

Listen and choose the correct response.

1. Do you have curly hair?
2. Are you married?
3. Does he have brown eyes?
4. Do you have a brother?
5. Do you usually go out on weekends?
6. Is your husband heavy?
7. Do you live in the city?
8. Do you have short hair?

Page 89 Exercise H

As you listen to each story, read the sentences and check yes *or* no.

Jennifer and Jason

Jennifer and Jason are visiting their grandfather in California. They're sad today. Their grandfather usually takes them to the park, but he isn't taking them to the park today.

Our Boss

Our boss usually smiles at the office, but he isn't smiling today. He's upset because the people in our office aren't working very hard today. It's Friday, and everybody is thinking about the weekend.

On Vacation

When my family and I are on vacation, I always have a good time. I usually play tennis, but when it's cold, I play games on my computer and watch videos. Today is a beautiful day, and I'm swimming at the beach.

Timmy and His Brother

Timmy and his brother are watching a science fiction movie. Timmy is covering his eyes because he's scared. He doesn't like science fiction movies. Timmy's brother isn't scared. He likes science fiction movies.

Page 91 Exercise E

Listen and choose the correct response.

Ex. What are Peter and Torn doing today?

1. What do mail carriers do every day?
2. Where are you going today?
3. What do you do when you're scared?
4. Do you usually use a typewriter?
5. Where do you usually study?

Page 93 Exercise D

Listen and circle the word you hear.

1. Our teacher can speak French.
2. I can't play the piano.
3. He can paint houses.
4. My sister can play soccer.
5. They can't sing.
6. Can you drive a bus?
7. I can't read Japanese newspapers.
8. My son Tommy can play the drums.
9. Their children can't swim.
10. Can your husband cook?
11. We can't skate.
12. I can use a cash register.

Page 97 Exercise K

Listen and circle the words you hear.

1. We have to go to the supermarket.
2. My son has to play his violin every day.
3. We can use business software on our computers.
4. Boris has to speak English every day now.
5. I can't cook Italian food.
6. Apartment building superintendents have to repair locks and paint apartments.
7. That actress can't act!
8. Our children have to use a computer to do their homework.
9. Mr. Johnson can operate equipment.

Page 98 Exercise M

Listen and choose the correct answer.

1. I'm sorry. I can't go to the movies with you today. I have to go to the dentist.
2. I can't go to the party on Saturday. I have to wash my clothes.
3. I can't have lunch with you, but I can have dinner.
4. We can't go skiing this weekend. We have to paint our kitchen.
5. I'm very busy today. I have to go shopping, and I have to cook dinner for my family.
6. I can't see a play with you on Friday because I have to baby-sit. But I can see a play with you on Saturday.

Page 102 Exercise H

Listen and circle the words you hear.

1. I'm going to visit her this year.
2. I'm going to write to my uncle right away.
3. I'm going to call them this Monday.
4. When are you going to cut your hair?
5. I'm going to fix it next Tuesday.
6. We're going to see them this December.

7. They're going to visit us this winter.
8. I'm going to clean it at once.
9. We're going to spend time with them this August.
10. I'm going to wash them immediately.
11. You're going to see us next week.
12. When are you going to call the plumber?

Page 103 Exercise J

Listen to the following weather forecasts and circle the correct answers.

Today's Weather Forecast

This is Mike Martinez with today's weather forecast. This afternoon it's going to be cool and cloudy, with temperatures from 50 to 55 degrees Fahrenheit. This evening it's going to be foggy and warm, but it isn't going to rain.

This Weekend's Weather Forecast

This is Barbara Burrows with your weekend weather forecast. Tonight it's going to be clear and warm, with 60 degree temperatures. On Saturday you can swim at the beach. It's going to be sunny and very hot, with temperatures between 90 and 95 degrees Fahrenheit. But take your umbrella with you on Sunday because it's going to be cool and it's going to rain.

Monday's Weather Forecast

This is Al Alberts with Monday's weather forecast. Monday morning it's going to be cool and nice, but Monday afternoon wear your gloves and your boots because it's going to be very cold and it's going to snow! On Tuesday morning the skiing is going to be wonderful because it's going to be sunny and very warm!

Page 108 Exercise T

Listen and write the time you hear.

1. It's seven forty-five.
2. It's six fifteen.
3. It's four thirty.
4. It's nine fifteen.
5. It's midnight.
6. It's five o'clock.
7. It's a quarter to nine.
8. It's a quarter after eight.
9. It's one forty-five.
10. It's noon.
11. It's eleven thirty.
12. It's a quarter to three.

Page 113 Exercise G

Listen to the story. Fill in the correct times.

Every day at school I study English, science, mathematics, music, and Chinese. English class begins at 8:30. I go to science at 10:15 and mathematics at 11:00. We have lunch at 12:15. We go to music at 12:45, and we have Chinese at 1:30.

Page 114 Exercise B

Listen to the story. Put the number under the correct picture.

Everybody in my family is sick today.

My parents are sick.
1. My father has a stomachache.
2. My mother has a backache.

My brother and my sister are sick, too.
3. My sister Alice has an earache.
4. My brother David has a toothache.

My grandparents are also sick.
5. My grandmother has a cold.
6. My grandfather has a sore throat.
7. Even my dog is sick! He has a fever!

Yes, everybody in my family is sick today . . . everybody except me!

How do I feel today?
8. I feel fine!

Page 117 Exercise F

Listen and circle the correct answer.

Example 1: I study.
Example 2: I played cards.

1. I planted flowers.
2. I shave.
3. I cried.
4. I typed.

5. I work.
6. I shouted.
7. I clean.
8. I studied.
9. I fixed my car.
10. I paint.
11. I smile.
12. I cooked.

Page 126 Exercise I

Listen and choose the correct response.

1. When did you write to your girlfriend?
2. When does your neighbor wash his car?
3. Who did your parents visit?
4. Where does Irene do yoga?
5. When did your son go to sleep?
6. When do you clean your apartment?
7. Where did you take your grandchildren?
8. What did you make for dinner?
9. When does Carla read her e-mail?
10. When did you get up today?

Page 129 Exercise B

Listen and circle the word you hear.

1. My husband is thin.
2. She was very hungry.
3. They were tired today.
4. He was very energetic at school today.
5. My wife is at the clinic.
6. Their clothes were clean.
7. My children are very sick today.
8. My parents are home tonight.
9. He was very full this morning.
10. The Lopez family is on vacation.
11. Their neighbors are very noisy.
12. These clothes were dirty.

Page 131 Exercise E

Listen and circle the word you hear.

1. I wasn't busy yesterday.
2. We were at the movies last night.
3. They weren't home today.
4. Tom was on time for his plane.
5. It wasn't cold yesterday.
6. They weren't at the baseball game.
7. My friends were late for the party.
8. The doctor was in her office at noon.

Page 134 Exercise I

Listen and choose the correct response.

1. Where were you born?
2. Where did you grow up?
3. What was your favorite subject in school?
4. When did you move here?
5. What did you look like when you were young?
6. Did you have freckles?
7. What do you do in your spare time?
8. Did you have a favorite hero?

Page 137 Exercise F

Listen and circle the word you hear.

Ex. Is Jane rich or poor?

1. It was a nice day today.
2. My friends were thirsty at lunch.
3. Who is your favorite hero?
4. Were Mr. and Mrs. Parker at home last weekend?
5. My new couch is uncomfortable.
6. My cousins were late for their plane.
7. Before I met Howard, I was very sad.
8. Your children are very cute.

Correlation Key

Student Book Pages	Activity Workbook Pages	Student Book Pages	Activity Workbook Pages
Chapter 1		**Chapter 10**	
2	2–4 Exercises A–D	88	69
4–5	4–5 Exercises E–H	89	70–71
		90–91	72–73
Chapter 2		95	74
8–9	6	**Check-Up Test**	75
10–11	7	**Chapter 11**	
12	8–9	100	76–77
14	10–11	101	78–79
16	12	102	80
Chapter 3		103	81–82
18–19	13	**Chapter 12**	
20–21	14–17	108–109	83–86
24	18–19	110–111	87–90
Check-Up Test	20	**Check-Up Test**	91
Chapter 4		**Chapter 13**	
28	21	118	92–93 Exercise B
29–30	22–25	119	93 Exercise C–95
31	26	122	96–97
Chapter 5		123	98–99
36–37	27	**Chapter 14**	
38–39	28–31	128	100
40	32–33	129	101
41	34	130–131	102–103 Exercise I
Chapter 6		133	103 Exercise J–107
46–48	35–39	134–135	108–111
Check-Up Test	40	**Check-Up Test**	112–113
Chapter 7		**Chapter 15**	
56	41	142	114–115
57	42	143	116–117
58	43–44	144–145	118–121
59–60	45	**Chapter 16**	
61–62	46–49	150	122–123
Chapter 8		151	124–125
68–69	50–51	152	126
70	52	153	127–128
71	53	**Chapter 17**	
73	54–56	158	129
74	57–59	159	130
Check-Up Test	60–61	160	131
Chapter 9		161	132–133
80	62–63 Exercises A, B	163	134–135
81	63 Exercise C–66	**Check-Up Test**	136–137
82	67–68		